RESILIENCE AND SUCCESS

Rochelle Brock and Richard Greggory Johnson III
Executive Editors

Vol. 27

The Black Studies and Critical Thinking series
is part of the Peter Lang Education list.
Every volume is peer reviewed and meets
the highest quality standards for content and production.

PETER LANG
New York • Washington, D.C./Baltimore • Bern
Frankfurt • Berlin • Brussels • Vienna • Oxford

Kabba E. Colley & Binta M. Colley

RESILIENCE AND SUCCESS

The Professional Journeys
of African American Women Scientists

PETER LANG
New York • Washington, D.C./Baltimore • Bern
Frankfurt • Berlin • Brussels • Vienna • Oxford

Library of Congress Cataloging-in-Publication Data

Colley, Kabba E.
Resilience and success: the professional journeys of African American
women scientists / Kabba E. Colley, Binta M. Colley.
pages cm. — (Black studies and critical thinking; vol. 27)
Includes bibliographical references and index.
1. African American women scientists.
2. Women scientists—United States.
I. Colley, Binta M. II. Title.
Q149.U5C637   500.82'0973—dc23   2013011822
ISBN 978-1-4331-1511-0 (hardcover)
ISBN 978-1-4331-1510-3 (paperback)
ISBN 978-1-4539-1131-0 (e-book)
ISSN 1947-5985

Bibliographic information published by **Die Deutsche Nationalbibliothek**.
Die Deutsche Nationalbibliothek lists this publication in the "Deutsche
Nationalbibliografie"; detailed bibliographic data is available
on the Internet at http://dnb.d-nb.de/.

The paper in this book meets the guidelines for permanence and durability
of the Committee on Production Guidelines for Book Longevity
of the Council of Library Resources.

Table of Contents

Preface

This book is a labor of love, and is the outcome of a shared interest in gender issues in science and in the overall struggle of women for equality. As husband and wife, and as scholars with different research agendas—one with an interest in gender issues in science and the other in parental involvement in education—our paths finally converged in the form of a collaboration on this book. It is beyond the scope of this preface to go into the details. However, the short and sweet version is that after conducting a study on student acquisition of science process skills in a project-based science curriculum, I (Kabba Colley) discovered that the female student participants at the middle-school level were outperforming their male counterparts in the program. At the high-school level, the reverse was true. When the data was disaggregated by race, it was even more startling. African American female participants, at the middle-school level, were outperforming everyone. However, at the high-school level, they lagged behind their peers. This raised some red flags for me. I was determined to investigate this further to find out what explains this discrepancy, and also to see what I could do as an educator to contribute toward resolving this discrepancy. As life would have it, this exploration did not take place until further along in my career.

When I did pick up this research strand again, one of the thoughts that came to mind was that perhaps I should look at the academic and professional trajectories of African American women scientists. By investigating the academic and professional trajectories of African American women scientists, I thought, I might be able to shed some light on why young African American women were lagging behind their counterparts despite the fact that they started out doing very well in middle-school science.

In 2004, I was fortunate to receive a modest research grant from the American Educational Research Association (AERA)/Institute for Education Sciences to investigate the subject. At about the same time, Binta and I were volunteering as facilitators for an after-school science program that focused on urban youth; mostly African Americans, Latinos, and Asians. The program not only worked to inspire these students to pursue science careers as an option, but also included workshops to assist their parents in supporting their efforts.

Over the course of several long conversations over dinner about the AERA project, I came to realize that Binta's expertise in parental involvement and social studies would inform and enrich this investigation . . . and so began the collaboration. Full details of the study (survey) are covered in the book.

Upon completion of the study, we found that like most studies, there were limitations. For instance, because the study employed a survey research method, it provided only a cross-sectional perspective on the academic and professional trajectories of African American women scientists. With Binta's leadership, we were able to plan and implement a case study in which we invited some of the survey participants to share their stories of struggles and resilience on their paths to becoming scientists. With this rich data, and Binta's gift for analyzing and interpreting qualitative data, we were able to construct their full stories. We found a series of pathways or maps with exits and entrances that took our participants on a complicated journey to their final destinations of gaining their doctorates and entering the scientific professions. Their journeys were influenced by family, culture, class, race, gender, faith, geography, and most important, opportunities and serendipity. Even though the circumstances of African Americans today have changed compared to the Jim Crow and Civil Rights eras, none of their journeys were smooth, as these African American women scientists revealed in their stories.

This has been a truly collaborative effort, with each of us contributing based on our disciplinary, pedagogical, and research strengths. We immersed ourselves in the preparation of this book individually and collectively, over meals, during conversations with friends, and while traveling on vacation trips. In addition, despite the fact that we both agree that staying up late is not healthy for individuals our age, we pulled several "all-nighters" to make this book a reality.

Every story has a context. Ours begins with a general history of women in science (Chapter 2), followed by a review of national data on women and minorities in science in the US (Chapter 3 and Chapter 4). Next comes a discussion of what the research says (Chapter 5), and a report on a survey of African American scientists. We end with a case study of a subsample of the African American women scientists who participated in the survey, all seen through the lens of Critical Race Theory. This brings us back to young African American female students who may or may not know that they have a passion and a sense of curiosity befitting a future scientist. For many young African American and low-income women in the US, the resources and support necessary for becoming successful in school science are lacking, not because they live in a poor country, but because the leadership and political will to provide the resources and support needed for all children to succeed in science are missing or absent.

We embarked on this journey in hopes that the stories of these African American women scientists would not only shed some light on the discrepancy in science performance of young African American women, but would serve as an inspiration for families, teachers, principals, counselors, scientists, researchers, curriculum developers, community activists, college and/or university faculty, policy-makers, and all those interested in the struggle to recruit, prepare, and retain a new generation of African American women in science.

Kabba E. Colley, EdD
Binta M. Colley, PhD

Acknowledgments

This study would not have been possible without the initial funding from the American Educational Research Association (AERA)/Institute of Education Sciences (IES) Research Grants Program. The authors will forever be grateful for this support. Our thanks to Dr. Felice J. Levine, Executive Director of AERA, for her support throughout the grant period. A special thanks goes to the following colleagues for their input, advice, and suggestions: Drs. Eleanor Amour Thomas, Ira K. Thomas, Andrea Billics, Janice Jackson, Carol Lerch, Kevin Clark, and Sandra Harris. We also want to acknowledge the National Society of Black Engineers (NSBE) and the National Society of Black Physicists (NSBP) for their assistance in distributing our research instrument. Pamela A. Bivens of NSBE and Lawrence Norris of NSBP deserve to be noted here for facilitating the process and sharing information. We are grateful to Drs. Wesley B. Pitts, Nicole Grimes and Femi Otulaja for making it possible for us to experience what a rich afterschool science program for inner-city kids looks and feels like. Finally, we want to express our thanks and appreciation to Nancy Disenhaus, Roshanda Harris, Christopher and Marsha Givens, Ethenia "Tippi" Phillips, and John Steinberg.

CHAPTER 1
Introduction

The academic and professional trajectories that African American women scientists follow have not been well documented, and studies of women scientists generally overlook African American scientists and/or do not disaggregate data by race and/or ethnicity. African American women scientists have made important contributions to the development of the science, technology, engineering, and mathematics (STEM) fields in the US. Studying African American women scientists and their contributions to STEM fields will help inform how we recruit, prepare, retain, and renew young African American women in particular and young women in general, in school and college science. This chapter provides an overview of how this topic is covered in each chapter of this book.

The journeys of African American women scientists contain stories of resilience and success. Our book tells these stories with particular emphasis on historical, cultural, family, and community influences; academic preparation; professional training; research interests; challenges; strategies for success; issues of equity and discrimination in the work place; and philosophies and ideas about science.

As part of the process of preparing this book, we conducted a research synthesis to learn more about prior works or books that have been written about African American and/or Black women scientists in the United States. Our hunch was that there were not many, and we were right. Of the dozen or so books we found, with a few exceptions, all contained micro autobiographies of selected, accomplished scientists, describing their struggles and victories. These books also documented the contributions African Americans have made to science, and the difficulties they had to overcome. Most notable among these books were *Blacks in Science: Ancient and Modern* (Van Sertima, 1998); *Black Women Scientists in the United States* (Warren, 1999); *Sisters in Science* (Jordan, 2006); and *Black Women in the Ivory Tower: 1850–1954* (Evans, 2007).

Our book builds on these and other works, with particular emphasis on beginning and mid-career African American women scientists who have achieved success in their careers despite all odds. It describes and discusses data from a sample survey of African American women scientists. In addition, it explores in-depth interview data from a selected sample of the surveyed scientists.

The essential features of this book are that it presents the stories of African American women scientists using the framework of Critical Race

Theory (Bell, 1995; Delgado, 1995; Delgado & Stefancic, 2001; Ladson-Billings & Tate, 1995; Tate, 1997; Yasso, 2005), and employing a research design that drew on multiple methods. To put the stories of African American women scientists in their proper context, the book also includes a treatment of the history of women in science and the contemporary history of Black women in science. The book is structured around the following guiding questions: What are the personal characteristics and academic backgrounds of African American women scientists? What led them to careers in science? What academic trajectories did they follow? What professional trajectories did they follow? What factors contributed to their success in science?

The book consists of ten chapters organized around key topics. Chapter 1 gives an overview of each chapter in the book. Chapter 2 gives a snapshot of the evolution of women's position in society through history, in order to lay the foundation for understanding the position of women in science, and specifically Black women in science today. In Chapter 2 we explore the inroads women made in science through religious and cultural rituals, and then move to the contributions they made as herbalists to the field of botany. It was through these activities that many women organized, drew, wrote about, explored, and disseminated the systematic strategies used to understand the world at that time. From organizers and disseminators, and with a change in attitude about women's place in the world, many undertook, of their own volition, to become experts in the field. With the expansion of empire and the exploration of new lands, many women found their way out of domestic duty and into the field.

It is in this chapter that we begin to see how men began to dominate when they realized that science was not about systems, but was very dynamic. With this change, it then became unfeminine for women to engage in science as professionals. We then track how this attitude continued through the years to today, where women are fully engaged, yet still are not totally acknowledged as capable—as represented by the unfortunate remarks about the natural disposition of women not being suited to math and science that were uttered by the former president of Harvard, Lawrence Summers.

Chapter 3 deals with the contemporary history of African American women in science in the nineteenth and twentieth centuries. With the advent of slavery, most of the accomplishments of African women disappeared from the record. In order to justify slavery, people of African descent had to be dehumanized in order for Europeans to maintain the attitude that they adhered to good Christian ethics. Knowing that they had stolen peoples from cultures as rich as and older than what existed in Europe, education—reading and writing—were banned for fear that the African would rise again to take her or his place in the world. By the time slavery had truly taken root, even scientific theories (of the snake-oil variety) were put forward that supported the idea of slaves as subhuman based on pseudosciences like phrenology, and facial and body types.

Struggling in this miasma that impacted both women and men, women exhibited such resilience and determination that they risked their lives and the lives of their children to gain an understanding of this new culture through learning to read their words. By the end of the Civil War, this thirst for knowledge led to changes in public education and higher education, fostering a sense of purpose that has reverberated through African American culture to this day. In addition to their gender, and the oppressive practices already in place, African American women scientists rose above the racial challenges put in their way to allow for the flow of young African American women in science to move forward today.

Chapter 4 examines the records on the state of African American women scientists in the US at the present time, and the academic and professional trajectories they follow. Data from the National Science Foundation, National Center for Science and Engineering Statistics, Women, Minorities, and Persons with Disabilities in Science and Engineering website were used to create tables and graphs for the period 2001 to 2010. This chapter then gives a graphic display of the numbers view of the progress of African American women in science careers.

Chapter 5 begins with a review of the various theories of gender difference and/or inequality in science in particular and society in general that have been presented in the past, with an emphasis on their contributions, assumptions, and limitations. It also reviews recent research that takes the position that there are no gender differences, and that it is a misconception promulgated by the same forces that have oppressed women in science because of their gender. This chapter then presents a framework for studying race and gender issues in science.

Chapter 6 provides a description and rationale for the three methodological traditions employed in the book, namely, survey research, case study, and research synthesis. In addition, it includes a section that describes the framework through which much of this book was written—Critical Race Theory. This section gives a brief history of Critical Race Theory and the important perspective it brings to understanding issues of race and gender in the trajectory of African American women scientists.

Chapter 7 describes the survey and case study methodology used. We relied mostly on the assistance of Historically Black Colleges and Universities (HBCUs), national Black scientific associations, national Black women's associations, and word of mouth. Not all of the organizations were able to assist us with lists, due to confidentiality concerns.

Chapter 8 is devoted to the survey findings from the study. This chapter focuses on the outcomes of the survey research, using tables and graphs to represent the responses the participants recorded. It also includes an analysis of their written responses to open-ended questions that focused on factors that contributed to their success, as well as the challenges they encountered in the process.

In Chapter 9 we review a subset of the original respondents to the survey who agreed to participate in phone interviews to further our understanding of their career paths, and to include the stories of their trajectories from a more personal level. Their stories emphasize the resilience and determination needed to navigate the maze leading to success.

Chapter 10 offers our framework for success, and discusses what the implications of such a framework will be for policy and practice. It includes recommendations for universities and colleges that are training science teachers, offers strategies that can be used in K–12 schools, and describes the important role that community organizations play. The women who shared their stories also have a role to play as models for the young women coming up behind them, and in participating in activities promoting science to young women taking place in schools and local community organizations. This chapter also makes recommendations for the kinds of activities academic institutions can engage in to change the oppressive attitudes that allow women, and specifically women of color, to be marginalized.

Although the primary audience for our book is undergraduate and graduate students enrolled in courses on women studies, gender studies, and the history of science, the book will also be of interest to college faculty, scientists, policy-makers, community activists, feminists, professional scientific associations, and all those interested in the education and welfare of women and girls in the US and abroad.

Throughout this book the reader is reminded that we use the words Black and African American interchangeably. In addition, it is important to note that although this book is on African American women scientists, we view the word "scientists" as representing not one discipline but multiple disciplines, and ways of developing understanding of the natural and physical universe. Most of the data that our book is based on present scientists and engineers as a group that shares similar characteristics. We therefore reflect this relationship and interdependence of the two disciplines in our treatment of the subject of African American women scientists.

CHAPTER 2
History of Women in Science

Early on in the history of humans and the natural world, women played a major role in the advancement of the sciences. They were knowledgeable regarding rituals of healing, health, and embalming. The skills women learned were part of their roles as high priestesses in ancient cultures. This chapter presents a brief overview of that history in order to lay the context for the challenges women face today, and specifically African American women. Women's rise to prominence in modern society, however, is a recent phenomenon. For the past three decades, women have been written back into the history of science (Gronim, 2007). Their participation in reading, writing, and teaching scientific principles was key in the dissemination and understanding of the discoveries of the natural world. Their contributions were hidden in the shadow of a few famous men of the Scientific Revolution, and presented mostly from a Eurocentric perspective. With colonial expansion and exploration, women who were able to travel to other shores had more freedom than their European counterparts. The story starts in ancient times.

The antiquities

One chapter on the history of women in science can only present a small piece of the whole story. This chapter gives a brief, historical overview of the evolution of women's position in society, in order to lay the foundation for understanding the position of women in science, and specifically of Black women in science today. The story begins with the earliest writings about women in the antiquities, because it is not possible to discuss the history of Black women in science without first revisiting the antiquities and history which have led to women's place in the field today. As we evolved in hunter-gatherer societies, women were left to build and cement the foundations of those societies. They became the ones to tend to the rituals, and, as a result, gained power. Additionally, their ability to hold inside themselves a growing child and give birth only added to the sense of wonder, and imbued them with a mysterious force. This can be seen in the Paleolithic carvings of the Mother Goddess which "expressed a sense that the fertility which was transforming human life was actually sacred" (Armstrong, 1994, p. 5). In Egypt or Kemet, Van Sertima (1997) described how, in the 25th dynasty, the pharaohs made it a practice to install their female relatives as high priestesses of Amon at Theses, giving them access to the scientific process of mummification, and to leadership in key temple rituals. Ascendency in the temple was based on the female line, and women in these roles were given a great deal of respect.

According to Diedre Wimby (1997), "the foremost and most significant fact to bear in mind when dealing with the issue of women and leadership in ancient Kemet (Egypt) is simply that there was equality between men and women" (p. 36). However, she went on to point out that, although women dominated the temple society, the concept of rulership denied women the position of leadership. The power women possessed in religious rituals, however, was envied by the priesthood, and Sanchez (1997) described how, for instance, at Akhnaton's death, these powers were reduced when the priests reasserted themselves by refusing to accept the belief that a woman could bypass the priesthood as a mother-goddess. This pattern is one that would be repeated in almost every culture.

The belief in equality between men and women in Egypt can be found as we move forward to the rise of Christianity in this area. In approximately 400 AD, Hypatia, a mathematician, scientist, and holder of a chair in philosophy at the University of Alexandria, was considered a universal genius, according to Beatrice Lumpkin (1997). She "wrote and lectured on mathematics, philosophy, physics and astronomy" (Lumpkin, 1997, p. 155). Contrary to drawings (no images of her exist) that represent her as Greek, she was born into an Egyptian family, and was not bound to the traditions that prevented Greek women from moving freely in society and from engaging in the work that she did. Unfortunately, she was caught in the middle of a philosophical and political feud between the Governor of Alexandria, Orestes, and the Bishop of Alexandria, Cyril. As a Platonist, she did not convert to Christianity, and her influence on Orestes was considered the defining force in the conflict (John, Bishop of Nikiu, 1916). According to Lumpkin (1997), "In 415 A.D. a mob of Christian fanatics murdered Hypatia and dismembered her body, scraping the flesh from the bones" (p. 155). It is important to note that her death was not because of her position at the University of Alexandria as a woman, but was due to the fact that she had what was considered undue influence on the politics of an emerging Christian movement that was still pushing against a Platonic society. Her high profile in Alexandria and as a scientist, mathematician, and philosopher made her an easy target.

The role of women in early societies has consistently been connected to science through the healing arts and religion. With the rise of Christianity, and the demise of a culture of gods and goddesses, women's position in society as powerful guardians of tradition and ritual began to decline. Armstrong (1994) clearly described the decline in the status of women as the cult of one god that overcame a society of many gods and goddesses:

> Even though monotheists would insist that their God transcended gender, he would remain essentially male. . . . In part, this was due to his origins as a tribal god of war.

Yet his battle with the goddesses reflects a less positive characteristic of the Axial Age, which generally saw a decline in the status of women and the female. It seems that in more primitive societies, women were sometimes held in higher esteem than men. The prestige of the great goddesses in traditional religion reflects the veneration of the female. The rise of the cities, however, meant that the more masculine qualities of martial, physical strength were exalted over female characteristics. Henceforth women were marginalized and became second-class citizens in the new civilizations of the Oikumene. Their position was particularly poor in Greece, for example—a fact that Western people should remember when they decry the patriarchal attitudes of the Orient. The democratic ideal did not extend to the women of Athens, who lived in seclusion and were despised as inferior beings. . . . In the early days, women were forceful and clearly saw themselves as the equals of their husbands . . . but after Yahweh had successfully vanquished the other gods and goddesses of Canaan and the Middle East and become the *only* God, his religion would be managed almost entirely by men. The cult of the goddesses would be superseded, and this would be a symptom of a cultural change that was characteristic of the newly civilized world. (p. 50)

This change in the status of women has been recorded throughout the history of antiquity. As Islam began its rise, the Prophet fought for the rights of women to participate in education, business, and leadership (Armstrong, 2007). "Women were encouraged to play an active role in the affairs of the ummah, and they expressed their views forthrightly, confident that they would be heard" (Armstrong, 1994, p. 158). When women asked the Prophet why the Koran did not address women, "The result was a revelation that addressed women as well as men and emphasized the absolute moral and spiritual equality of the sexes" (Armstrong, 1994, p. 158). However, Armstrong (2007) explained that the Prophet's opponents used his controversial "attempt to improve the status of women" (p. 154), as a way to smear his character through rumors and gossip. His wives were insulted on a daily basis because of his attempts to raise the position of women in society, and to protect them, he even took them to battle with him. Through a revelation, the Prophet stated that visitors could ask anything of his wives, but must speak to them from behind a screen. Furthermore, they (his wives) could not remarry after his death and must wear *jilbab*, which referred to various garments, in a distinctive way, so they could be recognized in the street and avoid harassment. This revelation was meant to protect his wives after his death, not subjugate all women.

Three generations after the Prophet's death, these words were used to require the veiling of all women. His remonstrations to treat women equally were marginalized and in some cases abandoned, and this revelation regarding permission to come to his wives' quarters was misinterpreted in a way that subjugated women and hid them away, more in line with what his opponents were used to in terms of older tribal traditions. As a result, the position of women in Islam has less to do with the Prophet Mohammed and more to do with a resistance to radical change and a level of comfort that the men felt with old ways. Armstrong (1994) summed it up well with this:

> Unfortunately, as in Christianity, the religion was later hijacked by men, who interpreted texts in a way that was negative for Muslim women. . . . The Koran does not prescribe the veil for all women but only for Muhammad's wives, as a mark of their status. . . . By the time of the Abbasid caliphate (750–1258), the position of Muslim women was as bad as that of their sisters in Jewish and Christian society (p. 158).

This, of course, is only a condensed version of the history of women in the ancient world. It does, however, highlight the thread of the inferior status of women that has been woven through the fabric of society for ages, and has exhibited itself in ways that have been hidden up to recent times. The same patterns can be seen in the evolution and history of the Catholic Church and the Holy Roman Empire, a topic not covered in this book.

The eighteenth century

This period was a time of expansion, empire, and discovery. Besides gold, silver, and gemstones, unknown species of plants and animals abounded in far-flung colonies, and each nation was anxious to find those flora and fauna that would increase the abundance of its empire in a sustainable and profitable way. Food production, this early on, was a major concern. However, there was so much new material being brought in through exploration, some order was needed.

The major players in this New World exploration were men. With the classification system developed by Linnaeus, it was now possible to order the world in what seemed a rational manner. The new field of botany was born, but women were barred from participating. The temptation was great, with the development of formal gardens, displays of plants and flowers in homes, and new and exotic plants coming in on the returning ships. However, in a male-dominated world, it was considered improper for a lady to indulge her curiosity in science (specifically botany), beyond the garden and flower arrangements, because Linnaeus's explanation for plant reproduction was based, in part, on human reproduction. Jane Marcet, a writer of scientific texts, agreed with the order of things, and made it clear that she considered herself an amateur. It was not suitable, in her view, for women to pursue professional training, because it was the purview of men (Leach, 2006). Once again the link between religion, science, and women's roles in the field was clear. For Christians in general, the roles of women were limited to domestic duties.

For Quakers, their religious beliefs were harmonized by the attitude toward science—both required observation and reflection. Because women played an equal role in the hierarchy of Quaker systems, there was no perceived conflict in their pursuit of scientific knowledge. Two such women were Priscilla Wakefield and Maria Hack. They specialized in scientific texts for children and young adults (Leach, 2006).

In the Netherlands (Jacob & Sturkenboom, 2003), the first women's society, "Women's Society for Natural Knowledge," was established in 1785 and ran through 1881. The women in this society were from the upper echelons of society, but were encouraged to seek the same understanding of the world as their male counterparts. Many of the records were destroyed in the bombings of Middleburg by the Germans during WWII. Ironically, their story is told from the records and diaries of the men who came to their meetings to lecture. The encouragement given to these women to pursue higher learning in the sciences is attributed, in part, to the philosophy of the Dutch Reformed Church—again making a clear link between science and religion. The pursuit of understanding the origins of life was no less than pursuing the vision of God.

These women were exceptions in terms of the support they received from their communities. For the most part, especially in the area of the study of plants, only the lowly peasant women who collected herbs and medicinals were immune from the isolation which Marcet advocated.

There are many women who defied the rules. One such woman who defied all the rules across gender, social status, and royal edicts, was Jeanne Baret, the mistress of an up-and-coming botanist, Philibert Commerson. According to Ridley (2010):

> a female botanist was a breach in the natural order of things. As the book of Genesis reminded Baret's contemporaries, it was Adam who was granted the privilege of naming what was found in Eden. When Eve aimed for more knowledge, the world changed forever. (p. 10)

The quote, again, presents the role of women in science as dictated by religion. However, Jeanne Baret was the first woman to circumnavigate the globe against the background of a royal edict banning women from traveling on ships. Disguised as a man, she risked her life and the status of her lover and the captain of the ship, in order to share in the adventure of collecting new species. Her contribution to the botanical collection of France was enormous, and Commerson took the lion's share of the credit. Her status as a woman was complicated further by her social status and relationship. She became the mistress of a man above her social class, was discovered by the crew of the ship to be a woman, and was gang raped and left, on her own, in Mauritius, for seven years after Commerson died. Through it all, she was able to marry a sailor she met while working as a barmaid, returned to France, and ended with a pension and the monies willed to her by Commerson. She was a botanist who gathered, pressed, organized, and labeled the collection that is still part of the Muséum national d'Histoire naturelle, with most of the credit going to Commerson.

As Ridley (2010) pointed out, there were other female botanical illustrators, like the Dutchwoman, Maria Sibylla Merian (1647–1717), who was encouraged to draw and paint by her father, and who changed the concept of spontaneous generation by observing and drawing the life cycle of moths and butterflies. According to Langenheim (1996), she was fortunate to have lived in the slave colony of Surinam for a period of time, where she contributed to the understanding of plant and insect cycles and diets. Although three volumes of her work were published (in 1679, 1683, and 1719) on *The Wonderful Transformation of Caterpillars and (Their) Singular Plant Nourishment*, she was considered an amateur, not a professional. As Langenheim (1996) pointed out, "Her accomplishments are the more incredible because women even in the nineteenth century had difficulty publishing anything other than popularized observations" (p. 3). She died a pauper, but her daughter published her work from Surinam posthumously. There was also the Englishwoman, Mary Delany (1700–1788), whose plant collages were valued and admired by male experts. Both Merian and Delany came from wealthy families. However, Baret was an early prototype of the peasant herb woman whose education of the male botanists made the collections we now know possible.

Although many of the women of these times made significant contributions to the sciences, they were tolerated and even, in some instances, encouraged, as they did not let their scientific endeavors interfere with their domestic responsibilities. Two women of note were Caroline Herschel and Mary Somerville (Gould, 2002). Herschel left Germany to join her brother, William, in England. He was an organist, and mentored his sister as a singer, but their musical careers were short-lived. William spent his spare time pursing astronomy. He also constructed his own telescopes. Just as he had tutored Caroline in music, she soon became his assistant as he scanned the skies. It is noted that she balanced this responsibility with her domestic duties and musical career. However, when William discovered the planet we now know as Uranus, he was granted a stipend of 200 pounds sterling by King George III. He was able to leave his musical work behind and focus on astronomy full time. Caroline dutifully followed, and became his apprentice. She developed complex mathematical calculations based on her brother's data, and, in 1786, she discovered her first comet. She continued to care for the household's domestic needs, even feeding her brother as he worked on his reflecting telescope. According to Gould (2002),

> The period 1786 to 1798 was a significant time in Caroline Herschel's life, we are told, not least given the marriage of her brother, William, in 1788. This apparently came as quite a blow to a woman who had thus far devoted her life to helping her brother. Nonetheless, now officially recognized as William Herschel's assistant and paid an annual salary of 50 [pounds sterling] from King George III, Caroline Herschel went on to discover seven more comets. She also embarked on a mammoth project to correct and cross-reference Flamsteed's authoritative star catalog, completing her index and list of omitted stars in 1798. (p. 1806)

It is interesting to note the large gap between what her brother was paid and what she was paid. Her acknowledgment did not end there, and will be discussed in the section on the 1800s. Mary Fairfax Somerville's work was also of the 1800s and will be included in the next section.

The exploration of the New World and colonialism was crucial to the history and evolution of the Scientific Revolution, according to Gronim (2007). In colonial New York, in 1752, Jane Colden studied the local plant life, and by 1756 had classified over 300 plants using the system developed by Carl Linnaeus. In 1756, she was the first woman to publish in a learned European journal a description of a previously unknown plant. Communications like this, from far-reaching places, changed the center of learnedness from Europe. As Gronim (2007) explained:

> And if the history of the Scientific Revolution was once almost exclusively a European story, historians have now demonstrated how crucial colonial places were to its development. The experiences of people who left Europe, and the huge volume of observations and specimens they sent back from all over the globe, forced European savants to reconsider their previous assumptions that all valid knowledge was contained in classical learning. . . . The model of the Scientific Revolution that now incorporates colonial places recognizes that, far from being one in which colonists sent raw specimens to Europe to be processed into knowledge, colonial people themselves were active producers of knowledge. (p. 34)

As with Caroline Herschel, Jane Colden knew "how to pursue her passion without transgressing the decorum deemed appropriate to women" (Gronim, 2007, p. 51). Her father played a major role in her botanical education, but in the end she even surpassed his skills and pursued the field not to please him but to please herself.

There were voices of women, at the time, who advocated for more freedom for women, like protofeminist writer Mary Wollstonecraft, who recommended in 1792 "that women receive a botanical education to promote both cultivation of the mind and greater awareness of the body. Wollstonecraft contrasted the female botanist with Eve in the Garden of Eden, arguing that the educated woman could maintain 'purity of mind' even when possessed of the 'fruit of knowledge'" (Gronim, 2007, p. 10). She published a lengthy plea for sexual equality titled, *A Vindication of the Rights of Woman*, which was published in French, English, Dutch, and German (Cohen, 1997). In this treatise, she demanded, "If women are to be excluded, without having a voice, from a participation of the natural rights of mankind, prove first . . . that they want reason" (Cohen, 1997, p. 141). Her response, and that of other feminists of this age, was provoked by the vitriolic opposition against women exercising equal rights that many men of this age held. Cohen (1997) described this phenomenon in the following:

> How important was the feared impact of the public discourse that had contested the alleged grounds for male supremacy during the previous hundred years? The alarm and hostility voiced by Nicolas-Edmé Restif de la Bretonne in 1796 may have been extreme, but it was not unrepresentative: "And so, I repeat to this century filled with error and folly, which seeks, despite nature, to confuse the two sexes in every way, man bears a greater resemblance to the male pig than to the woman who carries him in her womb, and in whose womb he places his son." (p. 141)

The positive side of all of this is that women "remained unconvinced and unintimidated" (Cohen, 1997, p. 141). They persisted in their engagement of political events, and continued to defend sexual equality regardless of the so-called scientific evidence during this era that proved that women had no capacity to reason or govern based on their anatomy and physiology (Cohen, 1997). As is clear, this belief from the eighteenth century is still alive and well today. It is a belief that impacts all women who have a passion for science, and, as we shall see, African American women specifically. The stories relayed here represent the tip of the iceberg, and women are finally being written back into the history of science and the development of "civilization."

The nineteenth century forward

These brief vignettes illustrate how the meme or thread of "women in their place" was woven into the fabric of human society from ancient times to today. However, it did not stop women from changing their status. In the 1800s, Marianne North crossed five continents in fifteen years, illustrating the flora she observed, and her watercolors are still displayed at Kew Gardens.

Many of the women who broke away (only to meet the ubiquitous glass ceiling) also came from privileged European or Colonial families. Returning to the story of Caroline Herschel (Gould, 2002), her productivity decreased until 1822 when she came to the aid of her nephew, John Herschel. He was engaged in astronomical studies, and she, once again, became the female helpmeet. She did, in her own right, complete a catalog of 2500 nebulae in 1828 which won her a gold medal from the Royal Society of London. Returning to Hanover, she consulted with many notable scientists, and was given an honorary membership in the Royal Astronomical Society. She was not the only woman to be so honored.

Mary Fairfax Somerville had an early interest and was self-taught in mathematics (Gould, 2002). Although her family did not discourage her endeavors, they merely tolerated her pursuit of knowledge. Her first marriage to Samuel Grieg smothered her attempts, but he died after three years and she was able to return to her studies. Her second marriage to William Somerville was fortuitous in that he shared her interests in math and science and "supported her thirst for knowledge. After all, she not once neglected her domestic duties" (p. 1806). With encouragement from her husband, she penned a paper on the magnetic properties of violet solar rays; translated and expanded Laplace's *Mécanique céleste*; and published papers in 1831 and 1843 titled, "Mechanisms of the Heavens" and "On the Connection of the Physical Sciences." She received recognition from the Royal Astronomical Society, and was elected as an honorary member to the Royal Irish Academy, which commissioned a bust of her for the Society's Library. She was given a pension of 300 [pounds sterling], one higher than William Herschel's, but probably representative of the cost of living at the time. Again, it is important to note that the support she was given was attributed to the fact that she did not desert her domestic duties as a woman. As Gould (2002) pointed out:

> So we have a picture of two diligent, well-behaved women. The blameless characters contrast sharply with the many men of science who have emerged from the archives with slightly grubbier reputations. . . ..
> Caroline Herschel and Mary Somerville, on the other hand, appear guilty of merely bending a few rules of etiquette, rather than outwitting their colleagues in the rush for recognition. Similar behavior from members of the fairer sex would doubtless have been frowned upon. Ladies at this time were expected to learn needlework, not nebular theory, and to amuse themselves by playing the piano rather than solving differential equations. Yet both our heroines appear to have navigated their way around possible objections with ease, silencing any possible dissenting voices by combining an appropriate model of dutiful, ladylike conduct with their scientific studies. Perhaps we should be applauding their skill in presenting a vision of domestic and scientific harmony, leaving critics of women's intellectual activity little or nothing to attack? (p. 1806)

As we have seen, women like Jeanne Baret laid the path, and she was not alone. According to Shteir (1996), between 1830 and 1860 academic botanists were working to reshape popular plant study into a science. Gender issues were crucial to this process, as botany was seen as a feminine, fashionable hobby, but scholars like John Lindley wanted to turn this "hobby" into a serious science. His first attack was on the Linnaean approach to naming and classifying plants. He favored the natural system of classification which focused on physiology and morphology. The Linnaean system was considered more a feminine approach to botany—something a mother could teach to her son as a beginning, before turning him over to men. As Shteir (1996) explained: "Their knowledge was situated and circumscribed, however, within gendered parameters. Thus, *A Sketch of the Life of Linnaeus* portrays a cultural field in which women give boys elementary training at home and then hand them over to men, who prepare them for adult responsibilities" (p. 30). Here, the bifurcation of botany begins with love of flowers being a feminine pursuit and the science of plans becoming a male pursuit. The Victorian Age heralded an emphasis on the social, moral, and spiritual value of botany, but also led to hierarchies of authority that, once again, edged women into the margins.

The role of women in science was also influenced by fashion. Ewing and Campbell Warner (2002) described the challenges of women pursuing science as aquatic biologists. They describe how Camelia Clapp at Mount Holyoke had her students dress in their gymnastics clothes to collect insects. She describes photographs of men easily wading in the water with their trousers rolled up over their knees or wearing hip boots, while women struggled to keep their hems from getting soaked because they were expected to wear skirts that covered their ankles. By the mid- to late-1800s, a major shift in attitudes toward women in science began to take place. According to Bergland (2008) women in science were seen as the gatherers, the orderers, those who recorded and labeled and organized the data in ways men were not capable of when science shifted from being systematic to being more dynamic. During the same time frame, efforts to define sexuality scientifically paralleled efforts to exclude women from science. Bergland gave this description from 1873:

> For example, Clarke (a professor at Harvard Medical School) argued that college-level education was dangerous to women's physiology. In *Sex in Education* he described the uterus as a delicate organ with a voracious thirst for blood. He claimed that college women thought too much and that their highly charged brains drew too much blood out of their systems, causing their sexual organs to shrivel away. As Clarke explained it, education was a "sterilizing influence" for women (Clarke 1873, 139). In fact, strenuous thinking could cause women to substitute "masculineness for

distinctive feminine traits" (45) and to risk becoming sterile, unwomanly creatures, "analogous to the sexless class of termites" (93). In Clarke's circularly antifeminist argument, women who argued for political or educational rights were those who had already "drifted into an hermaphroditic condition" (14) while only the woman who had "become thoroughly masculine in nature, or hermaphroditic in mind, "who had divested herself of her sex," could take a man's "ground and do his work" (115). (Bergland, 2008, pp. 81–82).

We can see from this passage that the work of Herschel and Somerville would not have been as valued had they not maintained their domestic duties and presented themselves as proper ladies who were also profoundly scientific. Most recently, during the run-up to the 2012 elections, we have had politicians who seem to hark back to Clarke's time, who believe that women's bodies have some "scientific" way of cancelling or preventing conception when rape is sensed by the body.

This pattern in the natural sciences was repeated throughout the nineteenth and twentieth centuries, and although there were major breakthroughs for women in science, it was an uphill battle. There were women like Marie Curie, (1867–1934) who benefited from the battle to equalize women's roles in science. Barbara McClintock (1902–1992), who received the 1983 Nobel Prize in Physiology or Medicine, was a distinguished cytogeneticist. Rachel Carson (1907–1964) is remembered for her environmental work and for the book, *Silent Spring*. Rosalind Franklin's (1920–1958) work and research led to the discovery of the structure of DNA, which Crick and Watson stole and were given credit for (Bleier, 1988). While her male counterparts shared information and socialized with each other, Franklin, the first woman to work in this laboratory, was isolated and patronized. The systematic subordination of women was embedded in the idea that feminine skills in science related to "work which is tedious, observational, computational, and taxonomic" (Bleier, 1988, p. 11). As discussed earlier in this chapter, women were the main disseminators of science in the 18th and 19th centuries. This continued into the 1920s with the fields of home economics and hygiene. Bleier (1988) explained:

> Traditionally, women scientists were the popularizers of science. Ellen Swallow Richards, the chemist from MIT and founder of the field of home economics, led other women scientists in arguing that science could teach wives and mothers nutrition, health, and hygiene. Richards was committed to teaching college women the domestic sciences to enable them to help solve the social problems around them. (p. 12)

Even though many of the women scientists were authorities in their fields, because the pattern of segregated employment became established, they did not receive any of the recognition accorded their male peers. Women in the male-dominated fields could be catalogers (that was feminine), but not researchers, discoverers, or faculty (that was not feminine). The situation was complicated by women advocating for feminine fields and women struggling to break into the male ranks. Bergland (2008) suggested that the infamous speech that the former president of Harvard, Lawrence Summers, made was retrogressive—to the mid-1970s, but may go back even further to the 1870s.

However, the thread of marginalization of women scientists goes back to the 1600s, according to some of the research cited here. Where portals of learning and of higher education in the sciences were open to women of European descent, for women of African descent the doors to this field were nonexistent due to over 300 years of slavery. The ancient records of their contributions were destroyed and/or ignored, and their acknowledged contributions are only now coming to light. In the next chapter, we will touch briefly on the ancient history, and focus on the contemporary history of women of African descent from the 1800s forward.

CHAPTER 3

Contemporary Educational History of African American Women in Science

In this chapter, we begin by looking at the legacy of slavery, the eventual emancipation of slaves, and how the history of the epoch still impacts the trajectory of African American women scientists. The pathway of education for White female scientists started in a much more rarified atmosphere than that for African American women. This pathway was not just about education, but about all of the other social and historical events of the past. The issue of education of African Americans in general begins with slavery and the fact that it was not only against the law for African slaves to be educated, it was punishable by death. This book does not cover the history of slavery, but it is important to note that at the beginning of trade between Africa and Europe, there was a principle of different but equal. The slave trade was so lucrative, however, that is was necessary to reduce Africans from human status to savages in order to justify the institutionalization of slavery. Davidson (1984) explained that those involved in the slave trade knew that equal but different was not feasible or sustainable:

> But the men with money knew better. . . . These were the years when a systematic and instrumental racism was born in Europe and America. . . . For racism was born out of the need to justify the enslavement of blacks. . . . From the first, racism was a weapon of exploitation. (p. 143)

In a later publication, Davidson (1985) described how, by the late 16th century, the superiority of Europeans became nascent. He explained:

> The degradation went beyond the slaving ships and plantations. Ramifying through European and American society, it formed a deep soil of arrogant contempt for African humanity. In this soil, fresh ideas and attitudes of "racial superiority," themselves the fruit of Europe's technical and military strength, took easy root and later came to full flower during the decades of nineteenth-century invasion and of twentieth-century possession of the continent. Even men and women of otherwise thoughtful and generous disposition came to think it well and wise that Africans should be carried into slavery . . . out of an "endless night of savage barbarism" and into the embrace of a "superior civilization." (p. 213)

Before they could even clear themselves of bondage, Africans were already tainted by the stereotypical belief that there was nothing from their cultures that inspired others to even consider them worthy of anything but hard labor and death. Slavery was deemed an improvement over the environment from which they had been abducted.

This attitude permeated American society to such a deep extent that even after the Civil War, it was not felt that former African slaves were educable. As a result, education for African Americans pre- and post-Civil War was problematic. Women, in general, had a difficult course to follow when it came to the sciences, but for those of African descent, the ascent was imbedded in a belief system that can be traced back to Kant—and maybe even further. Gates and McKay (1997) discussed the attitudes toward African Americans in terms of literature, but the same attitudes were held across disciplines. They explained in the following:

> Eighteenth-century writers privileged writing—in their writing about Africans, at least—as a principal measure of Africans' humanity, their capacity for progress, their very place in the great chain of being. As the Scottish philosopher David Hume put it in a footnote to the second edition of his widely read essay "Of National Characters":
>> I am apt to suspect the negroes, and in general all the other species of men . . . to be naturally inferior to the whites. There never was a civilized nation of any complexion than white . . . no ingenious manufacturers amongst them, no arts, no sciences. (p. 97)

These are the beliefs of the prevailing philosophers of the so-called Enlightenment. Neo-sciences popped up based on head bumps, facial features, and head sizes. The "scientists" who promoted these theories were supported and encouraged by a society that needed a way to keep African American men and women down. How could such a race aspire to education? These stereotypes sifted down through the ages, and to this day, and underlie the fear Whites have of educated African Americans. Another strategy, once slaves were moved as chattel into White society, was to destroy the proof, the idea that this was a people with a history. If you have no history, if you cannot root yourself in a culture—in advancement—of another time, you have nothing. Amadou-Mahtar M'Bow (1990), the former Director-General of UNESCO, articulated even more clearly how embedded this attitude was when he stated:

> Another phenomenon which did a great disservice to the objective study of the African past was the appearance, with the slave trade and colonization, of racial stereotypes which bred contempt and lack of understanding and became so deep-rooted that they distorted even the basic concepts of historiography. From the time when the notions of "white" and "black" were used as generic labels by the colonialists, who were regarded as superior, the colonized Africans had to struggle against both economic and psychological enslavement. Africans were identifiable by the colour of their skin, they had become a kind of merchandise, they were earmarked for hard labour and eventually, in the minds of those dominating them, they came to symbolize an imaginary and allegedly inferior Negro race. (p. viii)

This deeply embedded attitude is a memory gene or meme that is passed from one generation to the next as surely as genetic material passes from parents to their children. It has shaped the kind and quality of education available to African Americans to this day. It is only a recent phenomenon that Black History has become part of the historical record of human history. However, once African Americans were psychologically broken by the constant harangue from White society that they were nothing, it took immeasurable strength to break free and move forward.

The nineteenth and twentieth centuries

In general, formal education for African Americans was nonexistent. Most efforts consisted of secret, underground learning by those who had the fortune of learning to read the Bible. Evans (2007) described the four periods of slavery as identified by Carter G. Woodson: 1619 to 1750 as the solidification of slavery; 1750 to 1800 after the American revolution brought some relaxation of educational restrictions; 1800 to 1830 saw a backlash created by the Haitian Revolution and slave revolts; and finally, from 1830 to 1860 the struggle for emancipation intensified but the educational opportunities were fairly rare, even with the many formal and informal schools for Africans in America. Other limiting factors included geographical location. Most of the schools that offered college-level work that were open to African American students were in the Midwest. African American women were limited to the Literary Degree, and for African American men it was not much better. Evans (2007) described the most important of these: "The most notable were Oberlin (founded in 1833), Antioch (1852) and Wilberforce (1856), all in Ohio; Hillsdale (1844) in Michigan; Cheyney (1837) and Lincoln (1854) in Pennsylvania; and Berea (1855) in Kentucky" (p. 1). It is important to take a closer look at these schools, because they represent the general direction of education for African Americans pre- and post-Civil War. The main focus was teacher training, vocational training or mechanic arts, and agriculture.

Oberlin was established in 1833 (Oberlin University, 2012), by a Presbyterian minister and a colleague who was a missionary, to tame the pioneers of the westward expansion and bring a sense of Christian morality to what was seen as an untamed place. It was also one of the first higher education institutions to admit women and Blacks. Its main purpose was to train teachers and other leaders as pioneers headed west. Tuition was free, because students were expected to contribute to the building and maintenance of the campus. According to Evans (2007), the majority of the students came from the North and Midwest, and women were limited to the Literary Degree (LD). This was regarded as the "ladies course," as the bachelor's was considered more academically challenging and appropriate for men. Here we can see, once more, how the belief that women were inferior continued through the newly independent colonies. It was considered a fact that women were not capable intellectually to rise to the challenge, and that they were too delicate to be exposed to the rigor. Evans went on to explain that "The first black woman to attain the bachelor's degree did so two hundred years after a white male, forty years after a black man, and nearly twenty-five years after three white women received the B.A. from Oberlin in 1941" (2007, p. 25). Even so, Oberlin had enrolled 152 African Americans before the Civil War. These graduates became part of the foundation of educated African Americans, and opened the door to the dream of African American women pursuing professions in the sciences.

Antioch, another Ohio school, was established in 1852 (Antioch, 2012). Horace Mann, an abolitionist, was its first president, but Antioch, unlike Oberlin, was nonsectarian. It offered education to women and African Americans, again through an experiential cooperative work program. Of the schools, Wilberforce, established in 1856, was the first private, historically Black university in Ohio (Wilberforce University, 2013). With the state playing a major role in the Underground Railroad, Wilberforce provided a vaccine against the rule of ignorance during slavery. The school was originally founded by the Methodist Episcopal Church with great success early on. However, after the Civil War contributions dwindled and it closed its doors in 1862. Bishop Daniel A. Payne, an African Methodist Episcopal minister, petitioned to have the property turned over to himself and other members, as agents of the church, and the university was reincorporated in 1863. There were also schools established outside of Ohio that had a mission of including women and African Americans.

As mentioned above, they were Hillsdale in Michigan; Cheyney and Lincoln in Pennsylvania (Lincoln admitted women in 1952); and Berea in Kentucky. Hillsdale was established in 1844 as Michigan Central College in Spring Arbor (Hillsdale College, 2012). Although it was founded by the Free Will Baptists, it maintained a nonsecular philosophy, and was the first to prohibit race, religious, or sex bias in its charter. In addition to supporting the abolition of slavery, it was the second college in the nation to grant a four-year liberal arts degree to women. Cheyney was first established as the Institute for Colored Youth and was founded through a bequest of the Quaker, Richard Humphreys. Its mission was to train African Americans in education, mechanic arts, and agriculture so that they could compete with other immigrants who were arriving in the newly minted United States. As such, it was one of the oldest of the Historically Black Colleges. Of the schools highlighted, Berea had a unique history, as it was established in the South (Berea College, 2012). It was based on the Antislavery movement, a strong religious background, and the idea that equal numbers of Blacks and Whites would be educated together. They claimed an antislavery, anticaste, anti-rum and anti-sin institution. Many of its teachers were recruited from Oberlin in Ohio. Manual labor was dignified as a way to pay tuition, but before the school could establish itself it was driven from Madison County, Kentucky by pro-slavery sympathizers, and was not reincorporated until 1866. The first bachelor's degree was not granted until 1873.

Acceptance into a predominantly White institution did not guarantee a "wonderful life." The African American students at these institutions suffered insult, injury, separation of living and eating spaces, and lack of access to appropriate resources, but they struggled through because this era was fraught with the struggle to end slavery, and the need for those who were born free, escaped to freedom, or were yet to become free to get an education in order to further navigate a White-dominated society. Evans (2007) pointed out that most women "used words like joy, pleasure, or happiness to express their feelings about the learning process. Through constant pressures of psychological warfare, intellectual strain, public humiliation, or physical duress, they appreciated the exercise of learning enough to power onward" (p. 114). Even though most of the schools who admitted African Americans were good Christian schools, the religious beliefs of the founders did not mitigate the underlying meme that African Americans were inferior. In a 1901 *New York City Independent* article, Terrell defended Black women's rights to pursue a college education (Evans, 2007):

> in order to provide the utter worthlessness and total depravity of colored girls, it is boldly asserted by the author of *The American Negro* [W. H. Thomas] that under the best educational influences they are not susceptible to improvement. Educate a colored girl and white girl together, he says, and when they are twenty years old the colored girl will be either a physical wreck or a giggling idiot, while her white companion will have become an intelligent, cultured, chaste young woman. It would be interesting to know where the author of this book made his observations, or from what source he obtained his information. . . . I am also personally acquainted with colored women who have graduated from Ann Arbor University, Cornell, and the Chicago University, from Oberlin, Radcliffe, Smith, Wellesley, Vassar and other institutions throughout the North, South, East, and West, and not one of them is either a giggling idiot or a physical wreck. On the contrary, they are a company of useful, cultured women who would be a blessing and credit to any race. (p. 115)

Although Terrell came after many of the African American women pioneers at institutions of higher learning, it is important to understand that the abuse and humiliation they faced did not deter them from completing their goals. It is, even today, something that every college-bound woman hears: nothing is more important than an education. Once the doors to science education opened, as we will see, this philosophy, this belief was (and remains) the main driver of success for African American female scientists.

Many of the institutions established early on did not award degrees. The first college in the country to award degrees to African Americans was Middlebury College in Vermont (Evans, 2007). Alexander Lucius Twilight is recognized as the first African American college graduate, and received a BA from Middlebury. In 1823, a pastor by the name of Lemuel Haynes received an honorary MA from the same institution. However, Twilight is recognized as the very first. To give the scope of the limits of education for African Americans before the end of the Civil War, Evans explained that, "Approximately one hundred African Americans, including only three women, earned the B. A. before the war's end" (2007, p. 27). It should be noted that most of these graduates became educators. One of the exceptions was Norbert Rillieux, a quadroon, born to a French Engineer in New Orleans. His father, recognizing his talent, sent him to Paris to be educated in the early 1800s (Haber, 1970). Again, this was the exception, not the rule. By the mid-1800s, according to Evans (2007),

> black women in the North and South had opened schools to educate black people. Catherine Fergusun (1793) in New York; Julian Froumountaine (1819) and Miss DeaVeaux (1838) in Georgia; Sarah Mapps Douglass (1821) in Philadelphia; and a group of French-educated Haitian nuns in Baltimore (1829). (p. 27)

Sarah Mapps Douglass (Stewart, 1972) may have been one of the first to plant the seeds of scientific pursuit. Mapps was born in a prominent family of free African Americans in Philadelphia. She studied under private tutors, and in 1820 opened one of ten private schools available to Black children in Philadelphia. It was not out of financial need that the school was opened, but out of the deep belief that there was an obligation for those who could do so to engage in service to community. She was later responsible for the girls' department of the Institute for Colored Youth. It was at the Institute that she pioneered the introduction of scientific studies. These institutions were representative of the hundreds of African American women who taught their communities in an environment where it was illegal to do so. They set the bar high, and the bar was not coming down. Though in many of the schools the focus was on basic reading, writing, and arithmetic, these were skills necessary for African Americans in general and African American women in particular to move on to the sciences.

We find few Black women in science until the Civil War when many African American women, as refugees from the battleground and wards of the North, began to work as nurses. One of those was Susie Baker King Taylor, who had been marched to St. Simon's Island in Georgia (Bolden, 2004). Besides her work doing laundry, she also worked side by side with Clara Barton, the founder of the Red Cross. She was given the extra duties when it was discovered that she could read, a skill she developed through lessons her grandmother gave her covertly—lessons that could have cost her her life had her slave masters discovered this secret.

Bolden continued with the story of Mary Eliza Mahoney, who, during the same period, was working toward becoming the first African American registered nurse. Born free in Massachusetts, she worked "as a cook, janitor, washer-woman, and unofficial nurse's assistant, in 1878, at the age of thirty-three, she was admitted to the hospital's nursing program. Sixteen months later, she was one of the four in an original class of forty-two to make the grade in an intense course of class work and night-nurse duty" (Bolden, 2004, pp. 96–97). Mahoney, through the trials and tribulations of low-wage, low-level assignments, worked through the challenges to meet her goals. In 1976, fifty years after her death, she was inducted into the Nursing Hall of Fame.

The covert education of Taylor and the barriers placed on the path of Mahoney worked counter to the efforts put in place to prevent African Americans from getting an education. It became clear that if White society wanted to deny them this right, then education must be very valuable. Going to school became an obligation for African Americans, one that, even today, is repeated by parents, grandparents, aunts, and uncles—there is nothing more important than getting an education. It is important to note that especially in the South, during reconstruction, ex-slaves campaigned for universal, state-supported, public education (Anderson, 1988). The opposition to this movement was rooted in plantation society. Anderson stated:

> This uprising among former slaves was the central threat to planter rule and planters' conceptions of the proper roles of state, church, and family in matters of education. The South's landed upper class tolerated the idea of pauper education as a charity to some poor white children, but state-enforced public education was another matter. The planters believed that state government had no right to intervene in the education of children and, by extension, the larger social arrangement. Active intervention in the social hierarchy through public education violated the natural evolution of society, threatened familial authority over children,

upset the reciprocal relations and duties of owners to laborers, and usurped the functions of the church. (p. 4)

This opposition did little to stop the movement. According to Anderson, hundreds of so-called "native schools" and Sabbath schools were established, administered, and maintained by African Americans. Even Northern missionaries who went South to "save" the ex-slaves from illiteracy were astonished, and had to rethink the idea that African Americans were little more than uncivilized victims who were empty vessels into which they could pour the values and rules of civil society. The drive to attain higher education was firmly rooted in this early and successful movement. The change in education, in this case, was not just about opposition to the education of African Americans; it was also a threat to the social hierarchy established in the South that separated poor Whites from the plantation society. The advantage was to all of the poor, but especially to the newly freed slaves.

After the Civil War and during Reconstruction, there was a great deal of progress in terms of education for African Americans, but once Northern and Southern Whites became allies of sorts, the North abandoned its fervor for freedom and turned a blind eye as the South reinstated slave-like conditions through the enactment of Jim Crow laws. Litwack (1998) described the attitude clearly:

> Even as the debate persisted over the merits of such schooling, the opposition mounted in some areas made it a moot question. Speaking with "an intelligent business man," a visiting journalist was startled by the virulence of his reaction to an important black school in the vicinity. The school should be dynamited, he insisted, and the principal run out of the state. That, he explained, would force blacks to understand that ignorance, hard labor, and white domination constituted their permanent destiny. Although the visitor found the hostility contained in these remarks "incomprehensible," he did not find it exceptional. (p. 100)

For African American women, with the added burden of gender and race, it became something to fight for through and beyond contemporary times. The foundation laid by the "new woman," as elucidated by Hohl (2008), strengthened the resolve and resilience of the pioneers in the sciences. From nursing degrees to medical degrees, Georgia E. Patton was "the first African-American woman licensed physician and surgeon in Tennessee" (Bolden, 2004, p. 98). Patton graduated from Meharry Medical College in 1893. But she followed the trail of women who had graduated from medical colleges in New England, Pennsylvania, and Brooklyn between 1864 and 1891. It is with these women that the march of African American women into the halls of science began. This period of education paralleled the post-

Civil War Reconstruction Era, and many schools had been established to educate African Americans, especially Historically Black Colleges and Universities (HBCUs). Between 1837 and 1900 over 75 public and private Historically Black Colleges had been established, such as Cheyney University of Pennsylvania, the oldest public HBCU, founded by the Quakers as the Institute for Colored Youth (Cheyney University of Pennsylvania, 2012); University of the District of Columbia in 1851; Harris-Stowe State University in St. Louis in 1857; Clark Atlanta in 1865; Shaw University in Raleigh in 1865; and the list goes on. Many of these schools were originally founded as Normal Schools, but the impact of having this many choices at a time when there was none changed the face of the educated population in the United States. Religion played a major role in the establishment of many of the schools opened to African Americans, just as it played a major role in the will to survive and the belief that the climb must be made.

Education was seen as the only way for the race to progress. As difficult and humiliating as it was to enroll and finish in many of the institutions that were established for and welcomed African Americans, these schools were a microcosm of the events that were taking place in the wider community. The resilience needed for African Americans in general, and African American women specifically, was amazing. Lynching, loss of property, tarring and feathering, land loss, and the fight for civil rights was occurring at full tilt. Key to the determination and resilience of the women who would become scientists was the development of the "new" African American woman, the activist, the progressive. Hohl (2008) detailed the development of this new woman by focusing on the life of Ida B. Wells-Barnett. Using rhetorical analysis, life writing, and prosopography, Hohl (2008) outlined this development of the new woman in the midst of the general cultural shift. Prosopography is the collective study to determine the common characteristics of a historical group where individual biographies are not available. With access to education, African American women "were forging a wider space in which to act" (p. 7). This cohort of women began pre-Civil War and expanded after the Civil War, and they fought to maintain the history of the race as well as to defend and fight for the rights of African American women. At the same time, Hohl continued, White American women were also redefining themselves between the late 1800s and the 1920s, as the "New Woman" who could choose her mode of dress, partners, profession, and life. The antithesis was the "old" woman, who bowed to the tradition of the man as king in his castle.

The difference between the new White woman and the new African American woman was that the latter saw the "old" African American woman as someone who was to be respected and to whom they owed a debt for the determination to fight and survive. With the drive for education that developed in order for the race to become equal partners as free persons, this movement also provided support, information, and a network of strong new women that was as powerful as the suffragette movement. The sacrifice that these women made became the backbone, the ancestral support, that helped African American women who were struggling to get an education maintain their discipline and resilience. In addition to the backlash of Reconstruction, which heralded the establishment of Jim Crow and would bring the progress made not to a halt but to a crawl, there was also this society-wide resistance to the idea of an independent woman. For instance, Jim Crow allowed the passage of the Day Law in 1904 which forced Berea College—a school that was founded as a college for "Black and White together"—to decrease its racially mixed student population. This law prohibited integrated schooling in Kentucky (Evans, 2007). Changes in education were occurring against a backdrop of resistance to social and cultural change.

The 1900s saw an exodus from the South to the North of African Americans that fueled the Harlem Renaissance, fed the meat-packing industry of Chicago and other Midwestern cities, and kept the Second Industrial Revolution going between two world wars. These events required the skilled labor and education of more than teachers, nurses, and doctors, and were, in part, responsible for the fertile ground that led to the education of some of the first female scientists, in general. African American women still lagged far behind their White counterparts and even African American men, but the march forward continued. The most favorable opportunities existed at HBCUs like Spelman, where in 1919 photographs of the first African American women studying in science laboratories were taken (Jordon, 2006). According to Jordon (2006), a few African American women were involved in science as teachers and educators during the late 1800s and early 1900s, but it took another 30 years before Black women attained advanced science degrees.

However, these early "graduates with advanced degrees . . . were the shapers of curriculum, and they provided direction for a future generation of scientists" (Jordon, 2006, p. 6). Jordon (2006) explained that the advent of World War II created more opportunities for African Americans and for women. With men going off to war, it was easier for women and minorities to contribute their technical and scientific expertise. It also allowed for African American women like Ruth Moore to attain a PhD in bacteriology in 1933 from Ohio State, while Marguerite Thomas received her PhD in geology and Euphemia Haynes in Mathematics from Catholic University. These true pioneers and other trailblazers laid the foundation for African American women to continue their move into the sciences.

Just as the beliefs of Hume and Kant made indelible marks on the memories and socialization of Whites, the experience of African Americans, as they struggled to educate themselves and their children, also left indelible marks. Most African American families believed that education was a right to be pursued, even if it meant death. As history has found, many of the schools were dynamited, the teachers lynched, or at best, run out of town. This experience underlies and powers the determination of African Americans to seek an education, and is the fuel that empowered African American women to pursue a life of science. African American women faced multifaceted opposition to their rise within society, and especially within the sciences. Patricia Collins (1991) described this best as she defined the core themes from an African American woman's standpoint:

> All African-American women share the common experience of being Black women in a society that denigrates women of African descent. This commonality of experience suggests that certain characteristic themes will be prominent in a Black woman's standpoint. For example, one core theme is a legacy of struggle. Katie Cannon observes, "throughout the history of the United States, the interrelationship of white supremacy and male superiority has characterized the Black woman's reality as a situation of struggle—a struggle to survive in two contradictory worlds simultaneously, one white, privileged, and oppressive, the other black, exploited, and oppressed" (1985, 30). Black women's vulnerability to assaults in the workplace, on the street, and at home has stimulated Black women's independence and self-reliance. (p. 22)

To that assessment, resilience, perseverance, and determination must be added. These women rose out of a rich, activist, strong matrix that required them to succeed and thrive. As will be seen in later chapters, African American women, and specifically African American female scientists, not only struggled and survived, they thrived because of the generations of women who came before them and determined that education, at all levels, was key to progress.

Historical events impacted education for African Americans, and for African American women in particular. The Industrial Revolution, which had at its center iron, steam technologies, and textiles, had morphed into the Second Industrial Revolution, with a focus on steel, railroads, electricity, and chemicals. As the industrial focus changed from machines to science, more doors opened and the work of people like George Washington Carver received more attention. However, for women, there was still a struggle. Jim Crow was alive, well, and very strong during this period, but many fought on against the onslaught.

World War I, the scramble for and division of Africa by European powers, and U.S. dominance in North and South America widened the focus of policy-makers and the public on broader issues. This created another space for further moves into education and specifically the sciences—areas that had been closed and/or more difficult to break into. However, it is still the concept of struggle that, as the stories of African American women in science reveal, is a common thread on this path. The first woman to receive a PhD in the sciences was Flemmie Pansy Kitrell. Her doctorate was from Cornell University in 1936 in the field of nutrition (Titcomb, 1997). Born in 1907, Mary Elliott Hill earned her bachelor's in chemistry from Virginia State College in 1929. Another chemist was Gloria Long Anderson (Warren, 1999). She was the daughter of sharecroppers, born into a family of six in Arkansas in 1938. Her schooling started in an all-Black elementary school and continued in a training school or Black high school. She lamented that one of the losses of desegregation was an educational community, teachers who pushed their students, against all odds, to succeed. Her parents discouraged her from majoring in physical education or interior decorating, because they felt that doctors, lawyers, and teachers were needed. She enrolled at Arkansas A&M Normal College and majored in chemistry as a dare, and in 1968, after a long journey and encouragement from African American mentors, she graduated with her PhD in chemistry from the University of Chicago. She did say that although there was no organized harassment, the attitude of the faculty was that African Americans had been let in, but that expectations were low. Her dissertation was a study of fluorine-19 nuclear magnetic resonance substrate chemical shifts and CF infrared frequency shifts.

There are already many books written about these women, some in the form of lists that give only information about the educational track, and others that go into more depth. The point of recounting the history of their experiences, however, is to lay the context and background for the African American women spotlighted in this book. It is clear that family played an important role in terms of guiding these women to and through their careers. The history of struggle for education and the struggle against second-class citizenship fed into the next decades, and offered role models for modern African American women scientists. As important, and more difficult to articulate, is the bone-deep memory that because of the denial of education, because of those who fought, died, and struggled for justice in the African American community, African American women who make the decision to pursue advanced degrees in the sciences do so with an invisible posse always at their back. It is difficult to shut out the voices of grandmothers, great-grandmothers, and great-great-great-grandmothers who persevered so that these women could persevere and thrive. The best way to describe this is from lyrics by Y. M. Barnwell titled, "We Are . . .": "We are our grandmother's prayers. We are our grandfather's dreamings. We are the breath of the ancestors." This call, this memory, this meme is part and parcel of what has helped African American female scientists stay the course. The chapter that follows offers concrete evidence of how far these scientists have come, and also how far they have yet to go to create a critical mass in the field.

CHAPTER 4

Facts and Figures on African American Women in Science

We started this book by tracing the history of women in science and the contemporary history of African American women in science. Now that we have provided some historical context about the past, it is essential to take a look at the present. In this chapter, we will examine the records on the state of U.S. science in order to answer the questions: What do we know about African American women scientists in the US at the present time? What academic and professional trajectories do they follow? To answer these questions, we used survey data published by the National Science Foundation (NSF), National Center for Science and Engineering Statistics, Women, Minorities and Persons with Disabilities in Science and Engineering website: http://www.nsf.gov/statistics/wmpd/tables.cfm. The site published data tables on U.S. demographics, enrollments in science and engineering at the undergraduate and graduate levels, degrees awarded by levels, postdoctorates, and employment. Most of the data contained in the tables are reported by sex, race and/or ethnicity, and disability status, and cover the following periods: 2006–2010, 2008, and 2001–2010. To summarize and describe the data, we use analysis techniques and procedures for visualizing and communicating data suggested by Harris (1996).

The chapter focuses on the academic preparation of African American women in science and engineering as well as their participation in these fields. We concentrated on only data reported for the periods 2008 and 2001–2010. This chapter will also identify the leading institutions where African American women receive their education and training in science and engineering fields, and will describe their employment status, their representation in academic science, and the distribution of median salaries.

Because most of our analysis of the employment status of African American women scientists is based on data reported in 2008, our analysis on this variable has some obvious limitations. First, we do not have other years to compare. Second, not all the data reported is disaggregated by gender and race and/or ethnicity. So in cases where disaggregation by gender and race and/or ethnicity was not possible, we reported data on African American scientists and engineers as a group. It is also important to note that when we conducted our analysis, we decided to focus on selected science and engineering fields where the reporting of data was consistent over time. Specifically, we focused on biological sciences, physical sciences, mathematical sciences, and engineering. Our analysis did not include the social sciences, because the central characters of our book are African American women in the STEM fields. In some cases our analysis only looks at aggregated data of scientists and engineers because we could not find consistent and/or disaggregated data to tell the story with an emphasis on African American women scientists and engineers. In reading this chapter it is important to note that the names of categories or variables, methods of disaggregation, and reporting procedures change from time to time depending on new legislations and policies in place in Washington. However, despite these limitations, the data provide a valuable insight and a fresh perspective on the state of African American women in science.

Academic preparation

Baccalaureate degrees

Table 4.1 shows baccalaureate degrees awarded to African American women in science between 2001 and 2010. It is clear from the table that the bulk of the degrees awarded are in the biological sciences, computer sciences, chemistry, mathematics/statistics, and agricultural sciences, while the lowest number of the degrees awarded were in ocean sciences, astronomy, and atmospheric sciences.

In terms of trends over the decade under review, the awards of degree in the biological sciences showed an upward trend, while in the computer sciences, the trend was downward. In the agricultural sciences, chemistry, and mathematics/statistics the trend could be described as flat between 2001 and 2010 (see Figure 4.1 and Figure 4.2).

In contrast to Figure 4.1, Figure 4.2 shows fields where the least baccalaureate degrees in science are awarded to African American women. As can be seen, in atmospheric sciences, ocean sciences, and astronomy, the annual award of baccalaureate degrees in science to African American women ranges from 0 to 10. As for physics, the number of degrees awarded ranged from 29 in 2010 to 69 in 2002, with a trend line pointing downwards. The numbers for earth sciences are slightly lower than physics. However, the trend line for earth sciences seems to be moving upwards.

With regards to baccalaureate degrees awarded in engineering, Table 4.2 indicates that with the exception of aerospace and materials engineering, the numbers of African American women receiving engineering degrees (i.e., chemical, civil, electrical, industrial, and mechanical) is relatively similar from year to year. However, the trend line varies by field (see Figure 4.3).

The numbers of baccalaureate degrees awarded to African American women in chemical, electrical, industrial, and mechanical engineering are on

Table 4.1. Baccalaureate Degrees Awarded to African American Women in Science 2001–10

Field	2001	2002	2003	2004	2005	2006	2007	2008	2009	2010
Agricultural sciences	261	275	256	282	267	297	295	319	278	351
Biological sciences	3367	3357	3586	3723	3756	3972	4303	4376	4529	4501
Computer sciences	2027	2363	2845	2777	2383	2104	1624	1338	1330	1295
Atmospheric sciences	0	5	5	10	3	9	8	6	7	6
Earth sciences	23	20	21	29	33	21	29	38	26	33
Ocean sciences	1	7	1	1	2	0	1	0	2	0
Astronomy	0	1	1	2	3	4	0	3	0	2
Chemistry	513	519	489	510	508	558	548	575	592	582
Physics	43	69	41	62	57	49	43	45	43	29
Other	24	22	20	18	18	15	8	11	22	15
Mathematics and statistics	451	470	416	447	439	427	427	399	403	422

SOURCE: National Science Foundation, National Center for Science and Engineering Statistics, special tabulations of U.S. Department of Education, National Center for Education Statistics, Integrated Postsecondary Education Data System, Completions Survey, 2001–10. Arlington, VA: National Science Foundation.

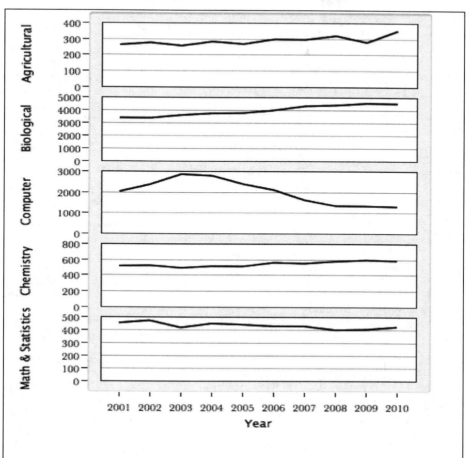

Figure 4.1. Baccalaureate Degrees Awarded to African American Women in Science by Field 2001–10 (Part I)

SOURCE: National Science Foundation, National Center for Science and Engineering Statistics, special tabulations of U.S. Department of Education, National Center for Education Statistics, Integrated Postsecondary Education Data System, Completions Survey, 2001–10. Arlington, VA: National Science Foundation

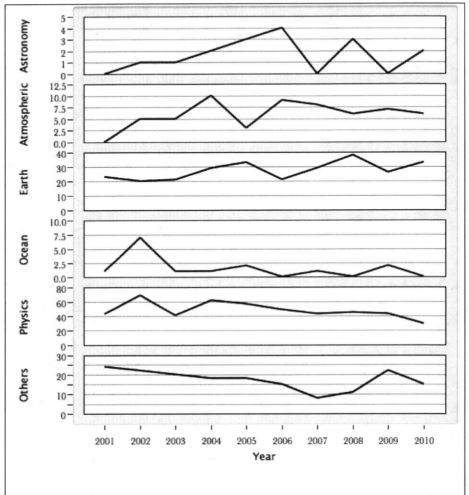

Figure 4.2. Baccalaureate Degrees Awarded to African American Women in Science by Field 2001–10 (Part II)

SOURCE: National Science Foundation, National Center for Science and Engineering Statistics, special tabulations of U.S. Department of Education, National Center for Education Statistics, Integrated Postsecondary Education Data System, Completions Survey, 2001–10. Arlington, VA: National Science Foundation.

Table 4.2. Baccalaureate Degrees Awarded to African American Women in Engineering 2001–10

Field	2001	2002	2003	2004	2005	2006	2007	2008	2009	2010
Aerospace engineering	8	9	17	12	10	19	16	20	21	16
Chemical engineering	194	190	168	154	152	130	128	122	122	118
Civil engineering	114	126	111	133	141	104	138	142	137	139
Electrical engineering	324	322	362	379	362	286	261	218	207	184
Industrial engineering	118	141	128	123	141	126	89	91	87	96
Materials engineering	11	20	9	14	11	14	10	13	13	9
Mechanical engineering	134	154	123	138	126	132	139	135	108	101
Other	125	129	145	148	141	175	184	156	163	142

SOURCE: National Science Foundation, National Center for Science and Engineering Statistics, special tabulations of U.S. Department of Education, National Center for Education Statistics, Integrated Postsecondary Education Data System, Completions Survey, 2001–10. Arlington, VA: National Science Foundation.

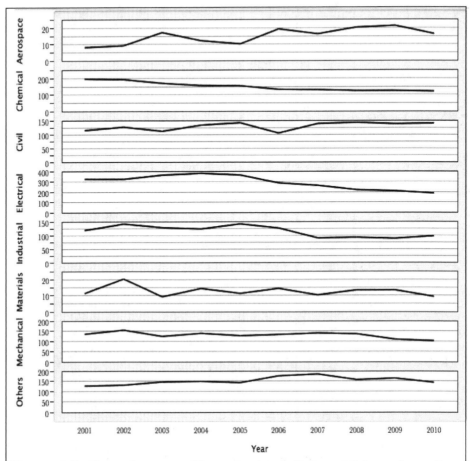

Figure 4.3. Baccalaureate Degrees Awarded to African American Women in Engineering by Field 2001–10

SOURCE: National Science Foundation, National Center for Science and Engineering Statistics, special tabulations of U.S. Department of Education, National Center for Education Statistics, Integrated Postsecondary Education Data System, Completions Survey, 2001–10. Arlington, VA: National Science Foundation.

the decline, while those in the fields of aerospace engineering and civil engineering show a relatively steady climb.

Master's degrees

At the master's level, African American women in science gained most of their degrees in computer science, followed by the biological sciences, agricultural sciences, mathematics/statistics, and chemistry (see Table 4.3). In the fields of atmospheric sciences, ocean sciences, and astronomy, there were very few African American women who chose these career paths at the master's level. Looking at Table 4.3, one could notice that the number of master's degrees awarded in these fields ranges from 0 to 5 annually. The small number of African American women graduates with master's degrees in atmospheric sciences, ocean sciences, and astronomy has implications for upcoming and future young African American women in science, because this means that there are few role models to learn from or look up to in these fields of science.

Figure 4.4 shows master's degrees awarded to African American women in science by field in the years 2001–2010. The trend line for the masters degrees awarded paints a different picture from the trend lines seen in the awards of baccalaureate degrees. For instance, while awards of degrees for biological and computer sciences are trending in opposite directions at the baccalaureate level, at the master's level, they are following each other upwards. An examination of Figure 4.4 also shows that the awards of master's degrees in agricultural sciences, chemistry, and mathematics/statistics are fewer compared to master's degrees awarded in other fields. However, it is fair to say that there were more African American women participating in the agricultural sciences in 2010 than in 2001. This is not true for the mathematical sciences, where participation at the master's level dropped in 2010 to the 2001 level.

The total number of master's degrees awarded to African American women in engineering between 2001–2010 is less than the total number of master's degrees awarded in the sciences (see Table 4.4), suggesting perhaps that there is more participation by African American women in science than in engineering. The engineering field with the most awards at the master's level is the field categorized as "Others" (see Figure 4.5). It is unclear what this category means. Perhaps it refers to nontraditional or emerging fields of engineering, such as computer engineering, network engineering, or software engineering. There is more participation by African American women in industrial, electrical, and civil engineering than in mechanical, chemical, materials, and aerospace engineering. Besides the category "Others," awards of master's degrees to African American women in industrial engineering have

Table 4.3. Master's Degrees Awarded to African American Women in Science 2001–10

Field	2001	2002	2003	2004	2005	2006	2007	2008	2009	2010
Agricultural sciences	51	49	65	59	59	61	77	62	74	77
Biological sciences	221	200	190	270	281	279	316	346	331	352
Computer sciences	331	335	407	416	363	354	345	385	355	463
Atmospheric sciences	1	0	0	2	1	5	3	2	2	3
Earth sciences	8	6	9	8	5	13	5	11	5	6
Ocean sciences	1	0	0	2	1	2	0	3	1	1
Astronomy	0	0	1	0	2	3	0	0	1	0
Chemistry	42	47	40	54	38	49	46	62	56	49
Physics	13	12	9	10	11	17	19	10	10	11
Others	4	6	2	3	3	3	5	4	4	5
Mathematics and statistics	48	64	49	52	60	78	76	81	71	48

SOURCE: National Science Foundation, National Center for Science and Engineering Statistics, special tabulations of U.S. Department of Education, National Center for Education Statistics, Integrated Postsecondary Education Data System, Completions Survey, 2001–10. Arlington, VA: National Science Foundation.

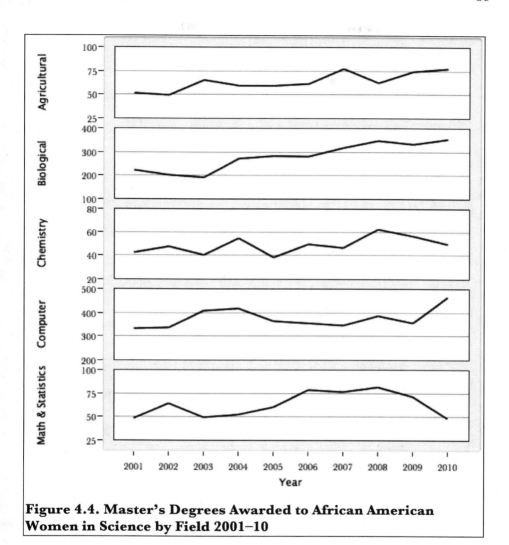

Figure 4.4. Master's Degrees Awarded to African American Women in Science by Field 2001–10

SOURCE: National Science Foundation, National Center for Science and Engineering Statistics, special tabulations of U.S. Department of Education, National Center for Education Statistics, Integrated Postsecondary Education Data System, Completions Survey, 2001–10. Arlington, VA: National Science Foundation.

Table 4.4. Masters Degrees Awarded to African American Women in Engineering 2001–10

Field	2001	2002	2003	2004	2005	2006	2007	2008	2009	2010
Aerospace engineering	2	0	0	1	2	3	8	3	4	8
Chemical engineering	19	12	20	14	24	12	17	17	9	11
Civil engineering	41	38	43	29	37	28	45	48	38	48
Electrical engineering	49	50	45	58	46	49	60	49	52	46
Industrial engineering	50	63	71	66	66	72	59	62	67	71
Materials engineering	2	12	7	11	9	4	3	6	8	7
Mechanical engineering	26	17	19	19	15	16	18	12	20	20
Other	56	71	76	86	83	95	92	98	106	123

SOURCE: National Science Foundation, National Center for Science and Engineering Statistics, special tabulations of U.S. Department of Education, National Center for Education Statistics, Integrated Postsecondary Education Data System, Completions Survey, 2001–10. Arlington, VA: National Science Foundation.

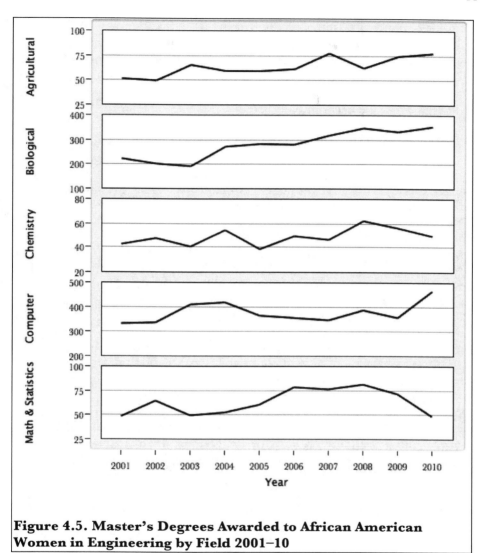

Figure 4.5. Master's Degrees Awarded to African American Women in Engineering by Field 2001–10

SOURCE: National Science Foundation, National Center for Science and Engineering Statistics, special tabulations of U.S. Department of Education, National Center for Education Statistics, Integrated Postsecondary Education Data System, Completions Survey, 2001–10. Arlington, VA: National Science Foundation.

also been showing an upward trend, increasing from 50 in 2001 to 71 in 2010. Similarly, the number in aerospace engineering, although very small, increased from 2 to 8 during the period under review (see Figure 4.5). From studying the award of master's degrees in engineering fields to African American women, one could conclude that participation at the master's level is lower than at the baccalaureate level.

Doctorates

Between 2001 and 2010, the number of African American women awarded the doctorate in the biological sciences more than doubled, from 64 to 147. During this period, 2009 was the best year, with a record number of 166 recipients (see Figure 4.6). The number of African American women receiving their doctorates in earth, atmospheric, and ocean sciences was disappointingly low compared to other fields, and was on the decline. Doctorates in agricultural sciences, although low, more than doubled during the period under review from 7 in 2001 to 30 in 2010. Doctorates awarded in the physical sciences showed an upward trend although there was a major decline in 2005. The participation of African American women in computer and mathematical sciences at the doctoral level was also disappointingly low, compared to engineering and biological sciences. For instance, between 2001 and 2010, the field of biological sciences awarded a total of 1,043 doctorates, engineering awarded 369, while computer and mathematical sciences awarded 83 and 74 doctorates respectively (see Figure 4.7).

Doctorates awarded to African Americans in science and engineering fields come from a diverse group of institutions, including public, private, Ivy League, and foreign institutions. However, the top ten institutions that award the most doctorates are Howard University, Spelman College, Florida A&M University, Xavier University of Louisiana, Hampton University, Morehouse College, Morgan State University, North Carolina A&T State University, Southern University and A&M College, and the University of Maryland, Baltimore County.

Employment status

According to the National Science Foundation (2008), there were 19.2 million employed scientists and engineers in the US in 2008. Approximately 10.7 million were males, 8.5 million were females, and 1.1 million were African American. In terms of age distribution, 35.2 percent of all employed scientists and engineers are between the ages of 50 and 75 years, 27.5 percent are between the ages of 40 and 49 years, 25.3 percent are between the ages of 30 and 39 years, and 12.1 percent are 29 years and below.

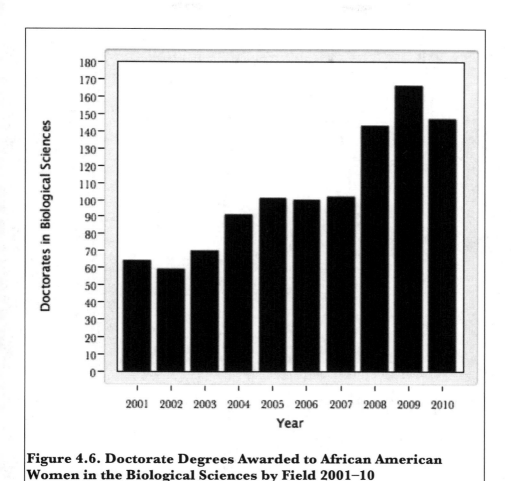

Figure 4.6. Doctorate Degrees Awarded to African American Women in the Biological Sciences by Field 2001–10

SOURCE: National Science Foundation, National Center for Science and Engineering Statistics, special tabulations of U.S. Department of Education, National Center for Education Statistics, Integrated Postsecondary Education Data System, Completions Survey, 2001–10. Arlington, VA: National Science Foundation.

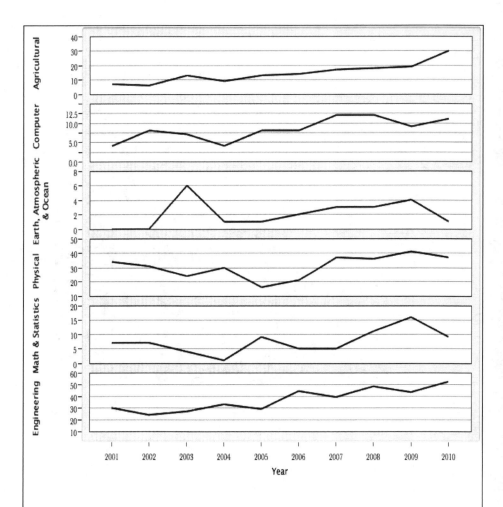

Figure 4.7. Doctorate Degrees Awarded to African American Women in Science and Engineering (With the Exception of the Biological Sciences) by Field 2001–10

SOURCE: National Science Foundation, National Center for Science and Engineering Statistics, special tabulations of U.S. Department of Education, National Center for Education Statistics, Integrated Postsecondary Education Data System, Completions Survey, 2001–10. Arlington, VA: National Science Foundation.

African Americans constitute about 5.8 percent of employed scientists and engineers, 7.6 percent of female scientists and engineers, and 4.3 percent of male scientists and engineers. The number of African American scientists and engineers unemployed or out of the labor force in 2008 was estimated to be 198,000.[1] Out of this number 33,000 were unemployed due to chronic illness or permanent disability; 29,000 because of family responsibilities; 26,000 were laid off; 109,000 retired; 41,000 did not need to work; 35,000 could not find suitable jobs; 20,000 were students; and 11,000 were classified as "others."

One of the rewards of being a scientist is receiving a decent annual salary or compensation for your work. Compared to other professions, the scientific and engineering professions paid very well. To determine how African American women scientists and engineers compare with their counterparts in terms of salary, we look at median salaries reported in 2008 in the following occupations: biology and life sciences, computer and information sciences, mathematical sciences, physical sciences, and engineering. It is important to note that our analysis did not include Native Indian/Alaskan Native and Pacific Islander because the data on these groups was unavailable or suppressed for confidentiality. In any case, we found that African American women in the biological and life sciences, and in physical sciences as a group had the largest median salary compared to their Asian, Hispanic, and White counterparts. However, in computer and information sciences and in the field of engineering, Asian women scientists had the highest median salary, followed by White women scientists and then by African American women scientists. In the mathematical sciences, African American women scientists followed Hispanic women scientists who had the highest median salary (see Figure 4.8).

In addition to analyzing the median salaries of women scientists, we also look at the median salaries of male scientists in the same occupations. Although there is variability by race and/or ethnicity, with Asian and White male scientists showing the highest median salaries (with the exception of the mathematical sciences), overall male scientists as a group had a larger median salary than female scientists (see Figure 4.9). This discovery is not new. For years, we have known as a society that women as a group were paid less than men for performing similar jobs with similar qualifications.

---

1 "Numbers are rounded to nearest 1,000. Detail may not add to total because of rounding and suppression, and because respondents could select more than one reason." (SOURCE: National Science Foundation, National Center for Science and Engineering Statistics, Scientists and Engineers Statistical Data System (SESTAT), 2008, TABLE 9-39).

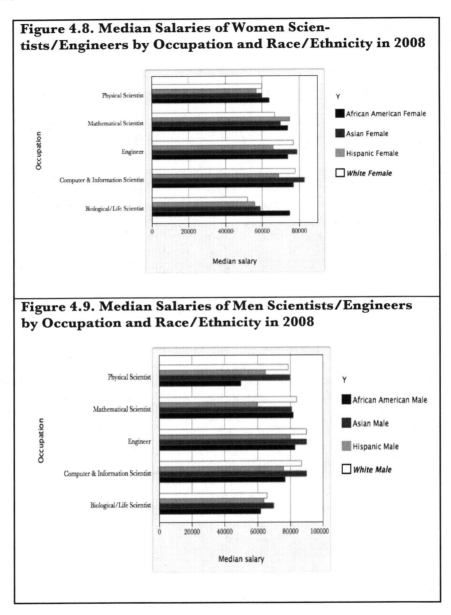

Figure 4.8. Median Salaries of Women Scientists/Engineers by Occupation and Race/Ethnicity in 2008

Figure 4.9. Median Salaries of Men Scientists/Engineers by Occupation and Race/Ethnicity in 2008

SOURCE: National Science Foundation, National Center for Science and Engineering Statistics, Scientists and Engineers Statistical Data System (SESTAT), 2008. Arlington, VA: National Science Foundation.

The Lilly Ledbetter Fair Pay Act passed by President Obama in 2009 is a step in the right direction, although more work on pay equality remains to be done.

In what sectors do most African American women scientists work? Who are their employers? To answer these questions, we look at data on employed scientists and engineers by sector of employment, broad occupation, gender, and race and/or ethnicity in 2008. We focused our analysis on two areas: employment in academic science and employment by sector.

Employment in academic science refers to employment in institutions of higher education (universities, four-year colleges, and related institutions). Figure 4.10 presents the percentage distribution of African American scientists and engineers in academic positions in 2008. It is important to note that the figure only presents the percentage of African American scientists and engineers and not the percentage of African American women scientists and engineers by academic positions. This is due to the fact that the available data reported by the National Science Foundation for 2008 was not disaggregated by gender and then by race/ethnicity. However, as mentioned earlier in this chapter, by extension, African American scientists and engineers also include women scientists and engineers.

An examination of the figure indicate that 52.3 percent held academic positions as teaching faculty; 28.1 percent as research faculty; 1.6 percent as presidents, provosts, or chancellors; 4.7 percent as postdoctorates; 9.4 percent as deans, department heads, or chairs; and 3.9 percent as adjunct faculty members. When we looked at the distribution of employment of the total population of scientists and engineers by academic positions, we found a similar pattern. For instance, based on the data reported in 2008, the majority of scientists and engineers working in academia were categorized as teaching faculty (49 percent), while research faculty accounted for 32 percent. President, provost, or chancellor positions accounted for 0.9 percent; postdoctorates for 5.1 percent; deans, department heads, or chairs for 8.0 percent; and adjunct faculty for 4.1 percent.

Although the distribution of African American scientists and engineers by academic positions in 2008 is similar to the distribution of the scientists and engineers by academic positions at the national level, the actual proportional representation of African American scientists and engineers in academic positions as a percentage of national total reveals unsettling figures. For instance, an analysis of data Table 9-22 (which is on science, engineering, and health doctorate holders employed in universities and 4-year colleges, by type of academic position, sex, race/ethnicity, and disability status in 2010), showed that African American scientists and engineers account for only 5.7 percent of presidents/provosts/chancellors, 4.8 percent of deans/department heads/chairs, 3 percent of research faculty, 3.8 percent of teaching faculty, 4 percent of adjunct faculty and 3 percent of postdocs (National Science Foundation, 2010).

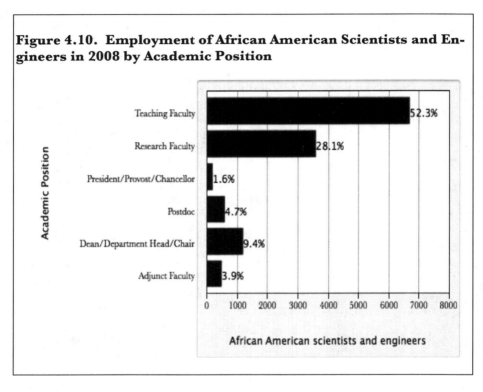

Figure 4.10. Employment of African American Scientists and Engineers in 2008 by Academic Position

SOURCE: National Science Foundation, Division of Science Resources Statistics, Survey of Doctorate Recipients, 2008 (preliminary data). Arlington, VA: National Science Foundation.

Figure 4.11 shows the distribution of employment of African American scientists and engineers by sector/employer. A review of the figure shows that based on the data reported in 2008, most are employed by business and industry, followed by universities and four-year colleges. However, when you look at and combine employment by state/local and federal governments, it totals 18.8 percent; government could therefore be considered as the second largest employer outside of business and industry. Employment of African American scientists by nonprofit agencies accounts for 6.8 percent, while self-employment accounts for 2.1 percent.

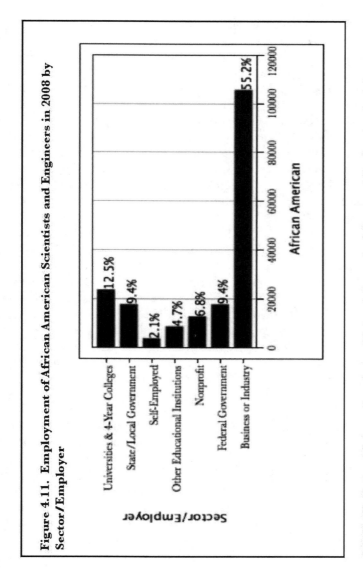

Figure 4.11. Employment of African American Scientists and Engineers in 2008 by Sector/Employer

SOURCE: National Science Foundation, National Center for Science and Engineering Statistics, Scientists and Engineers Statistical Data System (SESTAT), 2008. Arlington, VA: National Science Foundation.

Summary

In this chapter we set out to answer the primary question: What do we know about African American women scientists in the US at the present time? From our study of the data available, we learned that most of the baccalaureate degrees awarded to African American women in science are in the biological sciences, computer sciences, chemistry, mathematics/statistics, and agricultural sciences, while fewer degrees are awarded in the fields of astronomy, ocean sciences, and atmospheric sciences.

It is fair to say that at the baccalaureate level, the most common science degree awarded to African American women is the biological science degree. Degrees awarded to African American women in chemical, industrial, electrical, and mechanical engineering are on the decline, while those in the field of aerospace engineering and civil engineering showed a relatively steady climb. Awards in electrical engineering saw a decline of 43 percent in 2010.

Unlike awards of baccalaureate degrees, the awards of master's degrees in the biological and computer sciences are trending upwards. However, the total number of master's degrees awarded to African American women in engineering between 2001 and 2010 is less than the total number of master's degrees awarded in the sciences, suggesting, perhaps, that there is more participation by African American women in science than in engineering. Although it is unclear what the engineering field categorized as "Other" means, it is the field with the most master's degree awards. This suggests that African American women may be exploring new or emerging fields of engineering, rather than adhering only to the traditional fields.

With regard to doctorate degrees, awards in the biological sciences more than doubled from 64 to 147, with a record number of 166 recipients in 2009. There is serious underrepresentation in the awards of doctorates in earth, atmospheric, and ocean sciences. Furthermore, the trend in awards is downwards.

African Americans constitute about 5.8 percent of employed scientists and engineers, 7.6 percent of female scientists and engineers, and 4.3 percent of male scientists and engineers. As a group, African American women scientists in the biological and life sciences and in physical sciences have a higher median salary compared to their Asian, Hispanic, and White counterparts. However, in computer and information sciences and in the field of engineering, they trail behind. The overall analysis of median salary by gender revealed that male scientists had a higher median salary than female scientists regardless of race and/or ethnicity. This confirms what we already know about pay disparities in the scientific and engineering professions, and we will discuss the policy implications of this finding later in the book in Chapter 10.

From our analysis we learned that business and industry is the largest employer of African American (and by extension, African American women) scientists and engineers, followed by government agencies and universities and four-year colleges. In academic science, most are employed as teaching faculty. Only 28.1 percent are employed as research faculty. Less than 2 percent of African American women scientists are employed in senior executive or leadership positions. In academic science, employment with tenure carries more weight than nontenured employment. Opponents of the tenure process may disagree. However, in an uncertain job market, and given the politics of academia, tenure guarantees some people the academic freedom and security to pursue the scholarship that a faculty member wants without fear or favor. In any case, when we looked at the data on who gets tenure by science and engineering field and disaggregated the data by gender, we found that across the board, African American women scientists are grossly underrepresented in the ranks of tenured faculty (see Figure 4.12). Infact, in some fields, data is not reported (suppressed) because of low numbers. This underrepresentation has major implications for policy and practice, and we will discuss these further in Chapter 10.

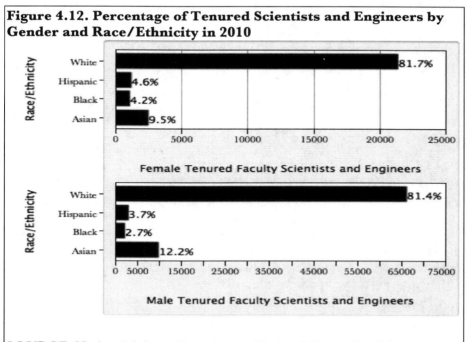

Figure 4.12. Percentage of Tenured Scientists and Engineers by Gender and Race/Ethnicity in 2010

SOURCE: National Science Foundation, National Center for Science and Engineering Statistics, Survey of Doctorate Recipients, 2010.

CHAPTER 5

What Research Says

Gender studies in science and math have supported the idea that there is a difference in the way males and females learn science and math. In this chapter we will review some of those studies and present studies that hold the opposing view—that there is no difference between male and female performance in science and math, but with a focus on science specifically.

Gender differences in school science

A number of studies on students' performance in school science have reported a gender gap. For example, an earlier report of National Assessment of Educational Progress (NAEP) (Mullis et al., 1994) noted that in 1992, male students had higher average science proficiencies than female students at ages 9, 13, and 17. The report further noted that, although these gender gaps have fluctuated from time to time, the differences were similar in 1969 and 1970. A study by Burkam, Lee, and Smerdon (1997), using the National Longitudinal Survey 88 database, reported gender differences in science achievement and science-class experiences. More recently, the National Center for Education Statistics' (2012) *Nation Report Card 2011* noted:

> Average scores for male and female students were higher in 2011 than in 2009. In 2011, male students scored 5 points higher on average in science than female students, which was not significantly different from the 4-point gap in 2009. (p. 8)

The Third International Mathematics and Science Study (Beaton et al., 1996; Keeves, 1992; Mullis et al., 1998) looked at broad issues in science education, including students' attitudes toward science, gender differences, effects of home background, equity, school effectiveness, and specialization in science. Data from over 20 countries including the United States were collected and analyzed. The key findings from the study revealed that gender differences in science exist in all but a few of the countries that participated in the study, and in all variables, and at all grade levels. The differences between male and female students increased with age, from 10 years old through the end of secondary school (Keeves, 1992).

With regard to science content knowledge, research findings from the NAEP studies (National Assessment of Educational Progress (NAEP) 1978a, 1978b, 1979a, 1979b) showed that there are gender differences among American students at both age 13 and age 17. A gender gap exists particularly in physical science, where males tend to have much higher scores than females (Burkam et al., 1997). Gender differences have also been found in biology and earth science, but the differences are smaller. In the section of the assessment that dealt with health and the environment, males scored higher in the environmental content area than females. However, in the health content area, females outperformed males. As far as science-process skills were concerned, there were no significant gender differences. Results similar to those of the NAEP were reported in England by Small and Kelly (1984a, 1984b) and Bransky and Qualter (1993), and in Israel by Friedler and Tamir (1990).

Some studies have examined the construction of high-school science achievement testing and its effects on gender. Linn, De Benedictis, Delucchi, Harris, and Stage (1987) found no gender differences on test items involving analytical process and multistep reasoning at ages 13 and 17. However, Hamilton (1998) found that gender differences exist on both multiple choice and constructed responses items, with females receiving lower scores than males on average. The researcher also found that there was a format effect, with the constructed responses favoring males. The largest differences were detected in items involving visual and spatial content and requiring the use of experiences gained outside of school.

Germann (1994) conducted a study to determine which of the following variables had the greatest effect on science-process skills: parents' education, preferred language, gender, science attitude, cognitive development, academic ability, and biology knowledge. The researcher studied 67 ninth- and tenth-grade biology students who lived in a rural community in New England. The data on science attitude, cognitive development, biology knowledge, and science-process skills were collected at both the beginning and end of the school year, and were analyzed using path analysis techniques. Findings from the study showed that cognitive development and academic ability had the greatest total effects on the acquisition of science-process skills. Gender was found to have no significant direct or indirect effect on science-process skills.

Some earlier studies have also looked at gender differences in student-teacher interaction in science classrooms (Baker, 1986; Brophy & Good, 1974; Davis & Meighan, 1975; Mayer & Thompson, 1963; Sadker & Sadker, 1986; Sears & Feldman, 1974; Stanworth, 1983; Tobin & Garnett, 1987), and have concluded that boys tend to have more positive interaction with science teachers than girls. Although the presence of a causal relationship between teacher interaction and science achievement is not certain, presumably having a greater interaction with teachers tends to help boys do better in science. Researchers such as Jones and Wheatley (1990) observed 30 physics and 30 chemistry classrooms (containing 1332 students and 60 teachers), and collected data on student-teacher interactions using the

Brophy-Good Teacher-Child Dyadic Interaction System. An analysis of their data showed that male students received significantly more teacher interaction than female students, as measured by the number of "call outs," "praise," "private contact," and "behavioral warning." Similar results were arrived at by Lee, Marks, and Knowles (1991) in a study of single-sex and coeducational secondary-school chemistry classrooms.

In Nigeria, Adigwe (1992) investigated gender differences in problem-solving in chemistry amongst secondary-school students. The sample consisted of 100 boys and 100 girls randomly selected from five rural and urban schools in Bendel state. The instruments used were free-response achievement tests, structured-response tests, a mathematics skill test, an attitude instrument, and a modified version of the Group Test of Logical Thinking. Analysis of the data was performed using a traditional t-test by gender. The results indicated that there were significant gender differences in problem-solving, particularly in problem understanding and representation, construction of problem-solving plans, exhibition of structural errors, execution of solution plans, and evaluation of solution process.

Mullis et al. (1994) studied trends in levels of science proficiency in the United States between 1977 and 1992. They categorized science proficiency into five levels: a level-150 child knows everyday science facts; a level-200 child understands simple scientific principles; a level-250 child can apply general scientific information; a level-300 child can analyze scientific procedures and data; and a level-350 child can integrate specialized scientific information. A comparison of proficiency level by gender revealed that 9-, 13-, and 17-year-old male students outperformed female students consistently at levels 250, 300, and 350.

The understanding of science concepts and their interrelatedness is considered an important variable in science learning (Shavelson, 1972; Shavelson & Stanton, 1975). Harty, Hamrick, Ault, and Samuel (1987), using a card game that tests students' competence in concept structure interrelatedness, found no gender differences in how male and female students construct and relate science concepts: "The result of this study, however, reflected that both boys and girls were relatively equivalent" (p. 113). Although Harty et al. (1987) did not observe any gender difference in the way boys and girls construct and relate scientific concepts, findings by Bransky and Qualter (1993) did find gender differences in physics concepts.

The type of community in which a school is located, or the socioeconomic status of the school, plays an important role in students' science achievement. For instance, Keeves and Dryden (1992) noted that "it is not uncommon within most countries for students from high status homes and for classrooms where the average level of aptitude is high, to be associated with schools with superior facilities and teachers" (p. 207).

Correlational studies conducted by Fleming and Malone (1983, r = .30) and Staver and Walberg (1986, r = .35) indicated that students' science achievement was not strongly related to socioeconomic status. However, Jones, Mullis, Raizen, Weiss, and Weston (1992) found that students from schools in advantaged, urban communities performed better in science than students from schools located in disadvantaged communities.

The proficiency level of female and male students in science has also been shown to be influenced by students' racial and/or ethnic background (Jones et al., 1992). In their survey of 20,000 American students in grades 4, 8, and 12, the researchers found that there were significant differences in science performance in grade 12, with African American and Hispanic females showing the lowest proficiency levels. Earlier studies by NAEP (1978b), Mullis et al. (1994), and Burkam et al. (1997) showed similar findings.

The relationship between gender, science content, and grade level was investigated by Steinkamp and Maehr (1983) through a synthesis of the literature. The authors found a small correlation between gender and science content for studies involving elementary-, junior-, and high-school students. Betsy Jane Becker (1989) conducted a reanalysis of Steinkamp and Maehr using meta-analytic procedures. In her summary of the results, she noted that

> "the reanalysis of results from Steinkamp and Maehr's earlier reviews indicated that subject matter indeed relates to the magnitude of science-achievement gender differences. Several other predictors, including school grade, do not appear salient" (p. 144).

Gender differences in planning and implementing science-fair projects at the childhood level (grades 1–6) were investigated by Adamson, Foster, Roark, and Reed (1998). According to the researchers, their aim was to examine an "elementary science fair through the lens of gender to discern if and how children's gender influenced how they do science in a context that is actively nonsexist and supportive of encouraging nascent interests in a variety of intellectual pursuits" (p. 851). They identified an elementary school that not only had a project-based curriculum, but also implemented science fairs regularly. The school also was known for encouraging its teachers to use innovative and nontraditional approaches to teaching young children. It was located in an urban area and had 20 percent minority students, mostly African Americans. Using a case study, Adamson et al. (1998) collected 268 students' projects over a two-year period. The first year they collected 107 projects produced by 129 or (56.1 percent) of the students. During the second year, they collected 161 projects produced by 193 or (74.5 percent) of the students. A group of 45 judges consisting of teachers, parents, and alumni (most with advanced degrees) was selected to judge the students' projects.

Students' projects were judged based on certain criteria that the researchers were interested in, and some were given merit or other types of awards. Upon analysis of the students' science-fair projects, Adamson et al. (1998) found that gender had no significant effect on participation rate for the first and second year respectively (Chi-Square = 1.21, p = 0.004). In terms of gender and field of science, they found significant differences, "with girls more likely to work within the area of social and biological sciences and boys within the area of the physical sciences" (p. 851). In addition to looking at gender and participation, and gender and field of science, the researchers also looked at gender and evaluation. In other words, was there a systematic relationship between gender and who evaluated a particular project? Their findings indicated no evidence that "gender affected how the projects were assessed." As part of the study, parents were asked to complete a survey, because the researchers wanted to learn about the effects of their participation and support on students' projects. They found that the

> Child's gender did not appear to influence parental responses to the survey. . . . Nor was gender salient in the lengthy comments that parents included on more than three-fourths of the 125 surveys. Common themes included the learning benefits of the fair, the difficulty of selecting a topic, and questions about the award system. Most parents also remarked on the intensity of feelings that the fair evoked. (Adamson et al., 1998, pp. 853–854)

In a recent study, Sorge (2007) investigated the relationship between age, gender, and science attitudes from elementary to middle school. Using a survey research method, the researcher studied students enrolled in a school-based science program in New Mexico. The sample consisted of 1080 students, of whom 595 were females and 485 were males, between the ages of 9 and 14 years. A science attitudinal scale consisting of 10 items scored on a Likert scale was used to collect data on students' attitude about science over a five-year period. Higher score on the Likert scale indicated a positive outcome. Each year students were pre- and post-surveyed at the beginning and end of the year. Data analysis, for reasons not well explained by the researcher, focused only on pretest data collected over a three-year period. Using descriptive statistics and a two-way analysis of variance, Sorge (2007) found that "Unmistakably a precipitous drop in science attitudes takes place between elementary and middle school" (p. 35). In addition, no significant effect was found between gender and age, although a significant effect was found between age and attitudes toward science ($F(5, 1068) = 46.88$, $p < .001$, partial $\eta^2 = 0.18$, $\eta^2 = 0.42$). In discussing the findings, Sorge (2007) reflected on the limitations of the study by citing demographic, social, and cultural factors as possible explanations. For instance, he claimed that New Mexico has a very different demographic (43 percent Hispanic or Latino, compared to 14 percent for the rest of the country); and that the number of persons living below the poverty line in this part of the country is 17 percent, compared to 13 percent for the U.S average. He also cited maturation of the students as a possible explanation for the drop in attitudes toward science. Unfortunately, although the findings are interesting and deserve some attention, Sorge (2007) did not explain the connection between demographic, social, and cultural factors, and a decline in attitudes toward science from elementary to middle school.

While Sorge's (2007) study focused on changes in attitude toward science that occur during the transition from elementary to middle school, Desy, Peterson, and Brockman (2011) looked at gender differences in attitudes toward science in middle and high school. Like Sorge (2007), they also used a 50-item survey instrument on a Likert scale. Some of the items were borrowed from other attitude-toward-science surveys. The survey focused on the following seven scales: perception of the science teacher, anxiety toward science, value of science in society, self-concept in science, enjoyment of science, motivation in science, and attitude toward science in school. Their sample consisted of 1299 students (316 males, 307 females, and 3 gender unknown were from middle schools; 326 males and 338 females were from high school; and 9 students who did not report their high school grade levels) taking science classes from six different school districts in southwest Minnesota. Descriptive and multivariate analysis of the survey data showed that there were no significant gender differences in attitude toward science for middle-school students, but significant gender differences were detected for high-school students. Students rated "enjoyment of science" and "motivation in science" the lowest, and "perception of the science teacher" and "value of science in society" the highest. Overall, female students reported more "anxiety toward science," less "enjoyment of science," and less "motivation in science" than their male counterparts. However, the researchers concluded by noting that "many of the females in our study expect to pursue a college major and subsequent career in a health related, science field" (Desy et al., 2011, p. 29).

From investigating the relationship between grade level, gender, and attitude toward science, researchers such as Bhattacharyya, Nathaniel, and Mead (2011) examined the influence of science summer camps on African American high-school students' career choices. Using a semistructured survey consisting of a 21-item science and career questionnaire, the researchers collected longitudinal data over a three-year period on a sample of 313 students ranging in age from ninth to twelfth graders (147 males and 166 females). They identified four variables which they thought influenced students' science attitudes, and these included parental involvement in schooling, previous and current science involvement, relevance of science to daily life, and perceptions of one's science academic ability. To determine whether students' attitudes changed over time and if that change was related to grade and gender, repeated measures analysis of variance was used. The results indicated that parental involvement in schooling and relevance of science to daily life had an effect on students' science career choices, while previous and current science involvement and one's science academic ability had no effect on science attitudes and career choices. In their conclusion, Bhattacharyya et al. (2011) noted:

> Overall, this study has found in the participants a mixed view of attitudes toward science. The students saw the value of science to society and the role of science beyond school, yet science was not a career preference because they perceived it as difficult. Many of them liked to perform science experiments but had no desire to be scientists. Gender seemed to be a crucial factor in choosing science as a career. Females tended not to choose science as a career as opposed to males. It was shown in this study that parental influences play a strong role in shaping girls' attitudes toward pursuing science as a career (p. 351)

Success in school mathematics is critical to success in school science because in most science subjects, students are required to use or apply mathematics principles and concepts. This is particularly true in physics and chemistry. A study of gender differences in school mathematics performance by Hyde, Lindberg, Linn, Ellis, and Williams (2008) looked at effect sizes across grades for U.S. mathematics tests, effect sizes across grades and U.S states, and percentage of children scoring above indicated percentiles and ratios. According to the researchers:

> Effect sizes for gender differences, representing the testing of over 7 million students in state assessments, are uniformly <0.10, representing trivial differences. Of these effect sizes, 21 were positive indicating better performance by males; 36 were negative, indicating better performance by females; and 9 were exactly 0. From this distribution of effect sizes, we calculate that the weighted mean is 0.0065, consistent with no gender difference. In contrast to earlier findings, these very current data provide no evidence of a great gender difference favoring males emerging in the high school years; effect sizes for gender differences are uniformly <0.10 for grades 10 and 11. Effect sizes for the magnitude of gender differences are similarly small across all ethnic groups. The magnitude of gender difference does not exceed $d = 0.04$ for any ethic group in any state. (Hyde et al., 2008, p. 494)

According to Huguet and Regner (2009), stereotype threat (ST), or the threat of being negatively stereotyped affects middle-school girls' performance in mathematics. In an experimental study, the researchers used a sample size of 199 middle-school students, 92 of whom were girls and 107 boys, with ages ranging between 11–13 years. The students were selected from eight French public schools in urban and suburban areas. In addition, the students came from diverse socioeconomic backgrounds. Students were placed in their regular classrooms, and each classroom was randomly divided into mixed-gender groups. Students were given a drawing and a geometry task, and told either the test would measure their ability in geometry or in drawing. The tasks were measured using a scoring rubric in terms of number and quality of units reproduced.

Student stereotypic-related beliefs were measured using a questionnaire. The boys were asked to rate the girls' performance in both tasks, and the girls were asked to do the same for the boys. Analysis of covariance of gender by task showed that there was a significant interaction between gender and task. With regard to the belief about the two genders' geometry abilities, girls expressed counterstereotype claims and boys expressed stereotype claims. A self-evaluation of their abilities revealed that girls self-evaluated their ability in geometry more negatively than boys, even though they had similar scores to boys. In the discussion of their results, Huguet and Regner (2009) noted that

> The present results are also of great practical significance. ST is found here in middle school girls from the general population, and who were similar to boys in their math grades, indicating that for teachers ST is indeed not necessarily visible at the surface. As suggested earlier in the present paper, teachers, but also parents and policy-makers, all may take for granted that elementary and middle school girls are not susceptible to ST, a fortiori when girls reject negative gender stereotype. (p. 1027)

The extent to which high-school physics preparation and affective factors predict performance in introductory physics at the university level was investigated by Zahra, Tai, and Sadler (2007). Using hierarchical linear modeling, they analyzed data consisting of 1,973 students representing 35 colleges, to answer the following question: "What high school physics curriculum, instruction, and affective factors predict female and male introductory physics performance after controlling for university course, demographic, and academic background variables?" Their findings showed that there were positive and negative predictors. The positive predictors included prior academic background and preparation in high-school physics, high-school English grades, high-school physics content, physics pedagogy, and high-school physics assessment. The negative predictors were some type of high-school pedagogy—namely, project-based science instruction, labs and demonstration, and microcomputer-based laboratories (MBL)—and family beliefs about school science. The fact that high-school pedagogies such as project-based science instruction, laboratory work and demonstration, and MBL were negative predictors of performance in university physics raises some alarm bells about how physics is taught at the university level and what physics knowledge, skills, and dispositions are valued. Project-based science instruction, laboratory work and demonstration, and MBL are inquiry-based science pedagogies, and the *National Science Education Standards* (National Research Council, 1996) emphasizes inquiry as the most effective way of teaching science. Studies of urban systemic science education reform enacted in the Detroit Public School System over a four-year period have shown that project-based science curriculum and instruction resulted in "significant and consistently high learning gains" (Rivet and Krajcik, 2004, p. 669). Similarly, Mokros and Tinker (1987) have found that MBL helped to improve students' understanding and ability to interpret graphs, a skill that is essential in physics and science in general. One would expect that because these inquiry-based science pedagogies mirror the way science is practiced in the real world, those students who are exposed to them would be more likely to succeed in science than those who are not. The findings are counterintuitive, and tend to suggest that there is a lack of alignment between high-school physics pedagogy and university introductory physics pedagogy, or that there is a much more complex problem.

Gender differences in academic science and STEM careers

During the last decade, there has been increased publicity both in the academic and mass media about the status of women in science. This increase in publicity could be due to several factors, such as the controversy sparked by the comments of former President of Harvard University, Lawrence H. Summers; the publication of major national reports on the status of women in academic science (American Association of University Women, 2010; American Federation of Teachers, 2011; Burrelli, 2008; Bystydzienski and Bird, 2006; Horning, 2003; National Academy of Sciences, 2010, 2007; Sonnert and Holton, 1995; West and Curtis, 2006); and the growing awareness of gender inequity due to the proliferation of new media. For instance, in 2004–2005, *The Chronicle of Higher Education* (2004, 2005a, 2005b) featured three articles on the status of women in science. The first article noted that despite the fact that more women are earning PhDs, their numbers are not growing in academia. The second article focused on the women in the National Academy of Sciences, while the third one presented the debate on gender difference in science sparked by Summers's comments. What is interesting about these articles is the lack of discussion about or mention of African American women scientists.

In a major volume subtitled, *Women in American Research Universities* (Horning, 2003), the advancement of women in higher education, the barriers they face, and the solutions being forged to overcome these barriers were discussed. However, no specific discussion was devoted to the contributions or experiences of African American women scientists. An earlier volume on women, gender, and science edited by Kohlstedt and Longino (1997) brought together philosophers and historians of science to discuss gender issues from their own perspectives. Yet, there was no discussion relating to African American women scientists.

The National Academies (2010) recently released a report titled, *Gender Differences at Critical Transitions in the Careers of Science, Engineering, and Mathematics Faculty*. The report, which was in response to a Congressional request, focused on three areas: academic hiring, institutional resources and climate, and tenure and promotion. Findings from the report (which are based on two surveys of 500 science departments and 1,800 full-time faculty) indicated that in some areas women scientists and/or faculty have made some gains, while in other areas, they still trail their male counterparts. For instance, the report noted:

> For the most part, men and women faculty in science, engineering, and mathematics have enjoyed comparable opportunities within the university, and gender does not appear to have been a factor in a number of important career transitions and outcomes . . . although women represent an increasing share of science, mathematics, and engineering faculty, they continue to be underrepresented in many of those disciplines. (National Academies, 2010, p. 5)

An earlier AAUP report (West and Curtis, 2006) indicated that gender differences still exist in academia, especially in relation to employment status, tenure, full professor status, and salaries. Using National Science Foundation (NSF) data, Joan Burrelli (2008) examined trends in employment of women faculty in science and engineering over a period of three decades (1973–2006). Her analysis showed that

> Women's share of full-time tenured or tenure-track S&E faculty increased over the period for which data on tenure status are available . . . these gains in tenured and tenure-track positions, as well as corresponding gains in full professor positions, reflect a rising inflow of female doctorate recipients in recent years, combined with nearly level numbers of men. (p. 4)

Evident from these three reports is that women have made some gains in STEM careers, although gender inequities still exist. It is also important to note that in all these reports, there was no mention of the employment trends, tenure status, and full professor status and salaries of African American female scientists and/or faculty, nor were the data used disaggregated to show how they compared with their counterparts.

According to Sonnert and Holton (1995), "women as a group receive fewer chances and opportunities in their careers and for this reason, they collectively have worse career outcomes" (p. 2). Testing this deficit-model-based theory, Settles, Cortina, Malley, and Stewart (2006) discovered from their study that women scientists who experienced gender discrimination and sexual harassment had negative job outcomes. In addition, the researchers noted that

> A few other interesting findings not central to the study's hypotheses were observed. In particular, women of color reported having less influence in their department than White women. Because they may experience multiple forms of discrimination and harassment, and they are likely to be racial tokens in their departments (and possibly also gender tokens), women of color may experience even greater social isolation than White women scientists. (Settles et al., 2006, p. 55)

The lack of attention to the issue of race in all of these studies on gender in STEM fields suggests that there is a knowledge gap and a lack of awareness of the interaction of race, gender, and science. This knowledge gap in the literature led scholars such as Adenika-Marrow (1996) to conclude that "Studies of women generally over-look women of color, and studies of students of color de-emphasize gender differences" (p. 80). According to Clewell and Ginorio (2002),

> the failure of research studies and national databases to disaggregate data on race/ethnicity and gender may be due to the tendency of researchers and policy makers to ignore people of color, but the sheer difficulty of working with small numbers may also be a factor. (p. 633)

However, the authors also noted that projected demographic changes are beginning to challenge this assertion, and assuming that the projections hold true, most of those who will be entering science will be people of color, and half will be women and girls.

Lewis, Menzies, Nájera, and Page (2009) investigated the monitoring and reporting of minority representation in the STEM fields by reanalyzing four nationally representative databases. In their findings, the researchers noted that there is a

> continuing need for research that identifies the factors that promote as well as limit the advancement of underrepresented minorities in science education and employment, and the pedagogical, institutional, and societal conditions that maintain the factors. Our findings also raise critical questions about how best to represent the trajectories of various racial/ethnic groups in the STEM disciplines. The inconsistencies across established databases in definitions of race/ethnicity, citizenship, and disciplines make it challenging to compare and integrate information and, in some instances, produce an illusion of progress. (p. 971)

There are emerging studies of the intersection of race and gender in science that employ innovative, yet rigorous qualitative approaches (Allen,

2003; Davis, 1995; Gilbert & Calvert, 2003; Russell & Atwater, 2005; Warren, 1999). To understand the academic and professional lives of African American women scientists, it is important to hear from them through their own voices. Jordan (2006) in her book, *Sisters in Science*, noted that

> African American women scientists want the same things all other scientists want: to be allowed to pursue and practice their science as freely and inventively as their imaginations and intellects will allow. On a human level, they want to belong and receive fair treatment in their dealings with others. Above all they want the same dignity and respect that any whole healthy person desires. (p. 236)

To describe the educational and career trajectories of low-income urban women who participated in Women in Science (WINS), an after-high-school program, Fadigan and Hammrich (2004) conducted a longitudinal case study using data collected from surveys, interviews, and program records of 152 program participants. In order to determine whether the women pursued their original educational and career goals and if elements of the WINS program influenced their decision-making, the researchers looked at the womens' educational and career trajectories before and after the program. In addition, they also examined the relationship between program components and their impact on the womens' educational and career trajectories. According to Fadigan and Hammrich (2004),

> Findings revealed 109 participants (93.16%) enrolled in a college program following high school completion. Careers in medical or health-related fields followed by careers in SMET emerged as the highest ranking career paths with 24 students (23.76%) and 21 students (20.79%), respectively, employed in or pursuing careers in these areas. The majority of participants perceived having staff to talk to, the job skills learned, and having the museum as a safe place to go as having influenced their educational and career decisions. (p. 835)

The researchers went on to say that

> These participants have grown into persistent women on a path leading them away from the poverty they have known for most of their lives, empowering them to break from a cycle that continues to trap far too many youth growing up in urban environments. (p. 854)

Instead of looking at underrepresentation of African American women in school science and the workplace, Julie Haun-Frank (2011) was interested in studying the science-career trajectories of African American students who were persistent in pursuing careers in science. The guiding questions for her research were stated as follows:

1. "What meanings of science, self, and science career did students construct as they traversed various spaces along their trajectories?"
2. "What critical spaces for identity work were evident in students' narratives?" and
3. "What role did these spaces play in their science trajectories?" (p. 241)

Using a case-study approach, a sample of fourteen African American high-school students attending an Early College High School Academy, and the theory of identity and social space as a framework, Haun-Frank (2011) found that across the group, the students expressed sustained interest, engagement, and enjoyment of science. Most of the students described themselves as being a "science person." They gave accounts of their childhood experiences in science, such as participating in an after-school program, school science experiments, and hands-on activities such as dissecting worms, as having an impact on their interest in science. In addition, they also noted that their science teachers influenced their career choices in science. Most of the students mentioned church as a physical space where they were introduced to science outside of the school through play and observation of surroundings. For instance, one of the students cited field trips to a zoo organized by their church. Haun-Frank (2011) also noted that the experience of injustices, particularly in the health-care arena, made the students even more determined to pursue careers in science as a way to address the injustices in their community. The students' families had a significant impact on their self-image and science-career choices, and contributed to their persistence in pursuing science careers. However, the researcher noted that the space of family framed their meanings differently. For instance, the researcher talked about the female students seeing themselves as caregivers and being more interested in health-related science fields, whereas the male students saw the space of family as a support and encouragement mechanism. The male students cited the popular media as a space for their identity formation. The students also gave accounts of the negative perceptions of society toward the African American male, and how this impacted their space in the community and school. They saw a future science career as a way out of their economic insecurity and as a pathway to a brighter future. In conclusion, Haun-Frank (2011) noted:

> Findings here suggest that students must be exposed to images and experiences that reflect realistic portrayals of scientists, the nature of their work, and varied employment opportunities. The resources students accessed (both in and out of school) did not expose them to multiple science-career trajectories. Both formal and informal science venues may be critical spaces to provide these opportunities. Finally, a spatial lens was critical for understanding the nuanced factors that impact

students' career decisions and pathways. This approach to the underrepresentation problem also raises other important questions related to the relationship between access and geography. In what ways are science and career resources spatially located, accessed, and put to use (or not) by particular groups and individuals in society? The more we learn about the spaces youth navigate, the better equipped we are to make available and support students' science-career trajectories. (p. 252)

Ley and Hamilton (2008) investigated the gender gap in the National Institutes of Health's (NIH) grant application data as a way to understand when and why attrition occurs in the MD and PhD biomedical pipeline. They conducted their analysis, which allowed them to determine the gender of applicants, funding success rate for different grants, and the different stages in the careers of biomedical scientists. They also looked at degrees earned by applicants, as well as their loan repayment and mentoring awards. They reported that in 2005, 49 percent of the 6,368 PhDs awarded in the biological sciences went to women. In addition, 49 percent of students admitted to medical school in 2007 were women. In the same year, the researchers noted, 51 percent of instructors at medical schools were women. However, there was a "striking drop" in the percentage of assistant, associate, and full professors who were women. In their conclusion, Ley and Hamilton (2008) wrote:

Our data show that career paths for men and women in biomedical sciences are different and that degree type influences career outcome. For the past several years, the numbers of female and male Ph.D. and M.D. students have been nearly equal, whereas female M.D./Ph.D. students compose about 40% of the total pool. (p. 1474)

The researchers went on to say that although some career attrition may be due to "cohort effect"—that is, small sample size entering a specific biomedical program—they warned that

Women make up an ever-increasing fraction of the students who train to become biomedical scientists, but their career attrition is disproportionate to that of men. If these trends continue, this country will probably experience a shortage of biomedical scientists in the near future. (p. 1474)

Although more and more women are entering higher education, their numbers are going down in science and engineering careers, according to a report by the Committee on Women in Science and Engineering (National Research Council, 2006) titled, *To Recruit and Advance Women Students and Faculty in Science and Engineering*. Two research questions guided the work of the Committee:

1. What are the more diverse institutions doing differently from their peers, which have seen small increases in the numbers and percentages of women? and

2. What is involved in the creation of diversity-building initiatives?

To answer their questions, the Committee conducted a review of the existing literature on programs and policies designed to enhance female participation in science and engineering fields, and visited four universities that had implemented successful approaches to advancing and retaining women students, faculty, or leadership, as determined by the numbers of students and/or faculty.

Findings from the study showed that women are still underrepresented in science and engineering; and among graduate students, postdoctoral candidates, and faculty. The report summarized the challenges to recruiting and retaining women in science and engineering careers as follows:

> Female students are less likely to take higher levels of mathematics prior to enrolling in college and are more likely to concentrate on the biological sciences or chemistry; female students have a less positive view towards successful study of science and mathematics; departmental cultures are more of an obstacle for women than for men; universities often lack female-friendly policies; students have negative perceptions of academic careers; postdoctoral candidates receive insufficient advising and mentoring during the graduate grogram; postdoctoral candidates have negative experiences during their graduate careers; postdoctoral candidates have individual preferences about career goals and views on the relevance of higher education; there may be bias against female postdoctoral candidates; female undergraduates, graduates and postdoctoral candidates face a variety of potential obstacles including: harassment, marginalization and isolation, attitude about career choice, lack of role models, and curricula perceived as less interesting or less relevant. (National Research Council, 2006, p. 111)

In looking at what the research says about gender differences in school science, we have learned that there are claims and counterclaims of gender differences in science, but in most cases the differences are extremely small and statistically not significant. In academic science and STEM careers, for most of the studies reviewed, very few disaggregate the data by race and/or ethnicity. Therefore, there is a knowledge gap with regard to how African American girls and women differ from their White counterparts. The collection and reporting of data on degree awards in science and on the participation of women, minorities, and persons with disabilities in STEM fields by the NSF and other federal agencies has given us more insight into how women and minorities are doing in some of the STEM fields. However, in school science, we still rely on studies that originate from different sources, vary in quality, and are limited in their generalizability to the broader population. Much more needs to be done to fill the gap in the literature as it relates to race and/or ethnicity and gender differences in science. An attempt is made in the next chapter to offer a strategy that fills part of that gap, including a discussion of Critical Race Theory and the role it plays in understanding issues of gender and race.

CHAPTER 6

Framework for Studying Race and Gender Issues in Science

Before presenting our framework for studying race and gender in science, we will begin with a review of the various theories of gender difference and/or inequality in science in particular, and society in general, that have been presented in the past. We will review some of these theories, with particular emphasis on their contributions to our understanding of gender issues in science, their assumptions, and limitations. A framework for studying African American women scientists will be proposed, and our rationale for selecting such a framework will be provided. In Chapters 8 and 9, we will demonstrate the application of our framework in the discussion of our findings.

Some scholars, such as Gray (1981), have suggested that gender differences exist in science because of biological factors. According to Gray, since gender differences in science achievement are present in all countries studied, and since little variation exists in the results of these studies, biological rather than environmental factors may be responsible for gender differences in science. The author argues that, although a gene for gender differences in science has not been discovered, studies conducted on rats and primates also showed that males consistently outperform females in solving complex spatial tasks (Buffery and Gray, 1972; Van Lawick-Goodall, 1968). This spatial ability, Gray noted, has been shown to predict success in quantitative thinking and performance on practical tasks, all of which are critical for success in science.

Kelly (1981) challenged the credibility of Gray's theory, and argued that the explanation for gender differences in science lies not with biology, but with the way that boys and girls are socialized in a patriarchal society. According to the author,

> Patriarchy should be understood as a principle which orders relationships between the sexes and between generations on specific lines—it divides home and work into masculine and feminine spheres, and into a hierarchy, with men in more powerful and prestigious positions where they exercise authority over women and children. (p. 59)

Kelly further argued that from the time that they are infants to the time they become adults, boys and girls are constantly being reminded of their gender through verbal and nonverbal communication from parents (Belotti, 1975); through toys (Stacey, Bereaud, and Daniels, 1974); through children's books

(Children's Rights Workshops, 1976); through science textbooks (Kelly, 1976); through the use of school facilities and space (Wolpe, 1977); through the school curriculum (Byrne, 1978); in attitudes of teachers toward boys and girls in the science classroom (Kahle, Parker, Rennie, and Riley, 1993); and through the mass media (Gill, 1977; McRobbie, 1978; Sharpe, 1976). All of these gender socializations and stereotypes affect girls' and boys' performance in science.

Saraga and Griffiths (1981) challenged both the Gray and Kelly explanations. They contended that girls' performance in science is too complex to be understood solely in terms of biological and social factors, and that "several factors must be integrated in a broader understanding of the social context in which science is carried out, and in which socialisation takes place" (p. 85). The authors noted that Gray's emphasis on spatial ability ignores other important factors such as anxiety, expectation, motivation, attitude toward science, etc., which are also understood to affect one's performance in science. In addition, they criticized Gray for using evidence from research on rats to explain gender differences in humans' spatial abilities. They considered this line of argument to be misleading because it ignored important differences between humans and animals, such as language acquisition and cultural transference, the capacity for learning, the capacity to change, the ability to develop new environments, and the division of labor. Saraga and Griffiths (1981) further argued that socialization in a patriarchal society is often seen as a one-way process, but this is not always true. They pointed out that girls and boys, at an early age, observe and construct their own rules about the world. They call this "self-socialization."

The position of women in society, Saraga and Griffiths (1981) claimed, is not only a result of social factors, but also of economic factors. They pointed out that in developed countries, regardless of political ideology and economic system, the division of labor is mostly based on gender. This means that men usually occupy the positions of power and influence, while women take over the role of producing and maintaining the labor force. The division of labor tends to put women at a disadvantage when compared to men. The fact that society is dominated by the male in turn affects the way that science is developed in society. According to Saraga and Griffiths,

> in advanced industrial societies, both capitalist or socialist, science is developed in relation to two major objectives. First, innovation is integral to increasing the efficiency of production through products and process improvement and change; second, it is integral to the development of the means of social control. Simply expressed, science develops in the service of the dominant interest in any society, both strengthening and defending them.

Sonnert and Holton (1995) put forward two models they believed explain why women are less likely to succeed in science, namely a "deficit model" and a "difference model." The deficit model states that "women as a group receive fewer chances and opportunities in their careers and for this reason, they collectively have worse career outcomes" (p. 2). The model assumes that women and men have similar goals, and that the only things preventing them from succeeding in science careers are structural barriers (legal, political, and social). They talked about formal and informal structural barriers. As an example of a structural barrier, they cited the example of admission rules at institutions of higher education that did not favor women or minorities before they were banned in the seventies and eighties, and mentioned discrimination in employment, tenure, and promotion.

The difference model says that women and men are different in their goals and aspirations and therefore "the obstacle to career achievement lies within women themselves; they are either innate or the result of gender role socialization and concomitant cultural values" (Sonnert and Holton, 1995, p. 3). This model assumes that some people are better than others in doing certain things because of their genetic disposition toward that thing. This model has been promoted by proponents of standardized testing, and has dominated the education system in the US for the past century. However, because of increasing research showing that women and men are more similar than we are led to believe (Barres, 2006; Gould, 1996), its validity today has been not only discredited, but also put in doubt by Janet Hyde (2005).

Hyde (2005) challenged the validity of the gender difference model by proposing the "gender similarities hypothesis." According to the researcher, "The gender similarities hypothesis holds that males and females are similar on most, but not all psychological variables. That is, men and women, as well as boys and girls, are more alike than they are different" (p. 581). To test her hypothesis, Hyde conducted a meta-analysis of research on psychological gender differences. Meta-analysis is a statistical technique used to summarize the results of many studies that investigated the same questions (Gay and Airasian, 2000). In a meta-analysis, the researcher organizes all the studies based on certain variables, and then uses statistical techniques to determine the effect size—that is, the difference between the means of the different study results. In her study, Hyde (2005) collected major meta-analyses that had been conducted in the past, including her own on psychological gender differences. She categorized the studies into six groups based on the variables they measure: abilities, verbal and nonverbal communications, social or personality, psychological well-being, psychomotor behavior, and miscellaneous constructs (moral reasoning). In addition, she made sure that the studies used were recent, and that their sample sizes were large. As far as effect sizes were concerned, Hyde (2005) hypothesized that most of the psychological gender differences she would find would be close to zero or small, a few would be moderate, and very few would be large or very large.

Her analysis showed that of the 124 studies whose effect sizes were estimated, 30 percent were close-to-zero or small, and 48 percent were in the small range. This means that roughly 78 percent of gender differences are small or close-to-zero. In discussing her findings, Hyde (2005) identified four key points to put her findings in perspective. The researcher noted that the gender similarities hypothesis does not mean that "males and females are similar in absolutely every domain" (p. 586), noting that there are exceptions, particularly in areas such as throwing velocity, sexuality, and aggression. Hyde (2005) went on to comment on the interpretation of effect sizes, noting, "the interpretation of effect sizes is contested" (p. 586). She added that current guidelines for interpreting effect sizes were set when meta-analysis was not invented, and that since then things have changed. There are different approaches to estimating effect sizes, and if one is not careful, there is a danger in making errors when one is interpreting effect sizes. She urged statisticians to take this into account as they work toward improving the method. Hyde (2005) also noted that "Not all meta-analyses have examined developmental trends and, given the preponderance of psychological research on college students, developmental analysis is not always possible. However, meta-analysis can be powerful for identifying age trends in the magnitude of gender differences" (p. 587). For instance, Hyde and her research colleagues found that in mathematics, it was originally held that around the age of puberty, boys were better than girls. However, when this was investigated, they found that there were differences in computation favoring girls in elementary and middle school, but no differences in high school. The importance of context was also included in the discussion of Hyde's findings. She cited examples, including the works of Claude Steele on stereotype threat, and described cases where the manipulation of context by the researcher resulted in a different outcome. Hyde (2005) ended her discussion by noting, "The question of the magnitude of psychological gender differences is more than just an academic concern. There are serious costs of overinflated claims of gender differences. The costs occur in many areas, including work, parenting and relationships" (p. 589).

As already noted in Chapter 5, the deficit model was put to the test by Settles et al. (2006) in a study of 208 faculty women scientists, designed to examine the effect of personal, negative experiences and perceptions of the workplace climate on job satisfaction, felt influence, and productivity. Using the method of hierarchical modeling, the researchers found that women scientists who reported poorer job outcomes also reported experiencing more sexual harassment and gender discrimination.

The nail in the coffin of the difference model was the work of Ben Barres (2006), who noted,

> Like many women and minorities, however, I am suspicious when those who are at an advantage proclaim that a disadvantaged group of people is innately less able. Historically, claims that disadvantaged groups are innately inferior have been based on junk science and intolerance. Despite powerful social factors that discourage women from studying math and science from a very young age 7, there is little evidence that gender differences in math abilities exist, are innate or are even relevant to the lack of advancement of women in science. (p. 134)

Barres's (2006) work is very relevant, and warrants discussion here, because for the first time in the field of gender and science studies, we see research that not only challenges the dominant theories of gender differences in science, but also signals a turning point in how we view the subject altogether. This is because Ben Barres is in a vantage position of not only being able to conduct research on the subject, but he also lived it. He is a renowned and distinguished Professor and Associate Chair of Neurobiology at Stanford University. Dr. Barres earned a BS in Life Sciences from the Massachusetts Institute of Technology (MIT), a PhD in Neurobiology from Harvard University, and an MD from Dartmouth College. He is also a female-to-male transgendered person. When he was age 14, he had an eye-opening experience, which he described as follows:

> I had an unusually talented maths teacher. One day after school, I excitedly pointed him out to my mother. To my amazement, she looked at him with shock and said with disgust: "You never told me that he was black." I looked over at my teacher and, for the first time, realized that he was an African-American. I had somehow never noticed his skin color before, only his spectacular teaching ability. I would like to think that my parents' sincere efforts to teach me prejudice were unsuccessful. I don't know why this lesson takes for some and not for others. But now that I am 51, as a female-to-male transgendered person, I still wonder about it, particularly when I hear male gym teachers telling young boys "not to be like girls" in that same derogatory tone. (Barres, 2006, p. 133)

Barres coined the term, "the Larry Summers Hypothesis"—the view that women are not progressing in science because of their inborn inabilities, rather than due to societal bias or external factors. According to Barres, this view is not only held by Larry Summers, former President of Harvard, but also by well-known scientists and scholars such as Steven Pinker, Peter Lawrence, Harvey Mansfield, and Simon Baron-Cohen, to name a few. He noted that all these men may be "well-meaning and fair-minded persons" who believe that people should be judged not based on race, ethnicity, gender, religion, or other classification, but based on merit. However, he questioned the validity of such a hypothesis, and noted that as a member of a minority group, he cannot help but be suspicious of people in positions of power who make disparaging claims about the powerless. Dr. Barres's research on gender differences in science, including a review of the available data and major studies on the subject, and his own personal experience and advocacy work on the subject, revealed that the claims do not add up. Barres found no supporting credible evidence to support the "Larry Summers Hypothesis." Instead, he put forward an alternative hypothesis, which he called the "Stephen Jay Gould Hypothesis." We shall paraphrase the "Stephen Jay Gould Hypothesis" as follows: that women in science are not progressing is not because of their "innate inability," but because of human, institutional, and societal forces over which they may have no control. In responding to the defenders of the Larry Summers Hypothesis, Ben Barres replied,

> Disadvantaged people are wondering why privileged people are brushing the truth under the carpet. If a famous scientist or a president of a prestigious university is going to pronounce in public that women are likely to be innately inferior, would it be too much to ask that they be aware of the relevant data? It would seem that just as the bar goes way up for women applicants in academic selection processes, it goes way down when men are evaluating the evidence for why women are not advancing in science. That is why women are angry. It is incumbent upon those proclaiming gender differences in abilities to rigorously address whether suspected differences are real before suggesting that a whole group of people is innately wired to fail. (Barres, 2006, p. 134)

Our review of the various theories of gender difference and/or inequality in science would be incomplete without touching on the feminist perspective on this matter. Feminist scientists were among the first group of scholars to bring to light the "gender issue in science," and to offer alternative interpretations of the scientific worldview and practice of science dominated by White men. For instance, in a critique of Western science, Keller (1996) noted,

> To see the emphasis on power and control so prevalent in the rhetoric of Western science as projection of a specifically male consciousness requires no great leap of the imagination. Indeed, that perception has become commonplace. Above all, it is invited by the rhetoric that conjoins the domination of nature with the insistent image of nature as female. (p. 36)

Yentsch and Sindermann (1992) investigated the challenges faced by women scientists in the workplace using questionnaires, interviews, small-group conferences, seminars, and conversations with colleagues. In their findings, they noted:

> Our study reaffirmed that women scientists' highest priorities are to advance ideas and knowledge, rather than to concentrate on rewards of dollars and recognition. However, this generalization should in no way obscure the need for equal access to all career benefits—tangible as well as intangible—regardless of gender. (p. 247)

In addition, the researchers cited Cole's (1979) "triple penalty" theory as the major barrier to women's progress in science careers. They include "(1) a cultural definition of science as inappropriate career for women, (2) a belief that women are less competent and less creative than men and (3) an actuality of discrimination against women in science" (p. 248).

In a recent article in the *Forum on Public Policy*, the journal of the Oxford Round Table, Unah and Dennis (2011) revisited Simone de Beauvoir's philosophical sexism and its implications for the debate on gender equality in Western societies. According to the authors, de Beauvoir's contribution to gender philosophy is her groundbreaking work on womanhood titled, *The Second Sex*, published in English in 1953. In *The Second Sex*, de Beauvoir distinguished between the concepts of "sex" and "gender," noting that the former is a biological characterization of the human species, while the latter is a result of sociocultural and historical processes. She raised tough questions about the condition of women, and offered a framework for equality and liberation.

Unah and Dennis (2011) made a compelling case for de Beauvoir's contribution to Western feminist theory, as demonstrated in the following excerpt from their article:

> The woman, Beauvoir argued, is a complete human being, just like the man. She is a free being, just as her male counterpart. She is capable of independent transcendence in creativity and work. As a free agent she can be said to exist only through the opportunities of her personal choices, living her own life, and bearing the responsibilities of her decisions. She, therefore, needs to be allowed the opportunities of this freedom, just like men. All social pre-designations that hinder this opportunity must be removed to enable woman to ascend her natural existential being; to enable and empower her to leadership. (p. 6)

In concluding their article, Unah and Dennis (2011) acknowledged the limitations of Beauvoir's project of "equality of the sexes," and noted that for it to be realized, men will also have to be liberated. The questions that one may ask are, "Liberated from what?" and "By whom?" Unfortunately, Unah and Dennis (2011) did not provide any answers to these questions.

Chiquita Howard-Bostic (2008) challenged the "wave analogy" that some feminists use to describe the history and origin of feminism in the US, because such descriptions are "both problematic and untenable to past and present roles of black feminist scholars and activists" (p. 1). According to her, the approach to understanding the history of feminism in the US that relies on the use of specific events as markers of peaks and troughs of women's struggle for freedom (wave analogy) is not only inadequate in explaining the Black feminist experience, but it is also exclusionary. To Howard-Bostic (2008), the wave analogy assumes that there is only a single feminist movement whose evolution followed a certain pattern. This is very misleading, and ignores the diversity and differences between groups and within the broader feminist movement in the US. She rejected the aggregating of this complex movement, including the "Black feminist agenda," into a "melting pot of feminist wave rhetoric," and advocated for a feminist movement that "embraces difference and allows for separate feminisms to dictate ways in which their separate paths complement and differ from one another. As difference is introduced, we will broaden trust, bridge knowledge gaps, and generate creative avenues for consensus" (p. 5).

In her book, *Black Feminist Thought*, Patricia Collins (1991) presented and argued for an Afrocentric feminist epistemology because according to her, Black feminist thought has been viewed by the mainstream academic establishment as "subjugated knowledge," and "Black women's efforts for self-definition in traditional sites of knowledge production" have been suppressed or have met with resistance. This has led Black feminist scholars to seek other avenues for their work, such as music, literature, and daily conversation. Collins (1991) offered five key dimensions of Black women feminists' standpoint. These include

1. Core themes,
2. Variation of response to core themes,
3. Interdependence of experience and consciousness,
4. Consciousness and the struggle for self-defined standpoint, and
5. The interdependence of thought and action.

The core themes refer to things all Black or African American women share in common, and that is the legacy of struggle and a culture of independence and self-reliance. Although Black or African American women share the core themes together, they do not all respond to them in the same way. Factors such as class, ethnicity, religion, region of the country, and sexual orientation produce diverse experiences for African American women, and may determine the type of responses to the core themes. Collins (1991) noted,

> Being Black and female may expose African American women to certain common experiences, which in turn may predispose us to a distinctive group consciousness, but it in no way guarantees that such a consciousness will develop among all women or that it will be articulated as such by the group. (p. 24)

The author also added that although African American women as a group may develop a certain type of consciousness that gives them a vantage "vision," translating this consciousness into a collective Black feminist standpoint poses a great challenge, because dominant groups oppose or often reject such standpoints. According to Collins (1991), one reason why standpoints of oppressed groups are usually opposed or rejected is because they provoke a spirit of resistance. A Black feminist standpoint must include all the key dimensions described above. In addition, it must combine thought and action, and reject the type of thinking that views the two as separate. Collins (1991) believed that it creates divisions among the oppressed groups, splitting them into "theorists" and "activists." She cited the examples of the contributions of Black women intellectuals in the nineteenth century, and how their consciousness was also informed by the struggle of poor, working-class Black women, such as the washerwomen. Because Black women have access to both feminist and Afrocentric epistemologies, an alternative Black women's standpoint, Collins emphasized, must reflect both traditions.

Critical social theory

As the above review has shown, the theories used to explain gender difference and/or inequality in science and society not only vary, but also are fraught with many unanswered questions. In our study, we have decided to settle for Critical Race Theory (CRT) (Bell, 1995; Delgado, 1995; Delgado and Stefancic, 2001; Ladson-Billings and Tate, 1994; Tate, 1997) as a framework for understanding race and gender issues in science. CRT draws from an interdisciplinary knowledge base that includes history, sociology, law, ethnic studies, and women's studies (Yasso, 2005). To understand Critical Race Theory, we must go back and trace its historical roots.

Critical Race Theory belongs to a family tree of critical theories called Critical Social Theory. Although theories of society and social theories critical of human society have been in existence since the beginning of the first human civilization, Critical Social Theory, as we know it today, is a modern phenomenon. Its origins can be traced back to the "Frankfurt School," an institute for social research that was established in Frankfurt, Germany in the 1920s. The purpose of Critical Social Theory is to critique and understand human society with the aims of promoting social justice and liberating human beings from oppressive and exploitative social relationships. According to Kellner (2010), the Institute's work was directed in the 1930s by Max Horkheimer, who wrote in the first issue of the Institute's journal, *Zeitschrift fur Sozialforschung*, that the purpose of their work was to develop a

> "theory of contemporary society as a whole," aiming at "the entirety of the social process. It presupposes that beneath the chaotic surface of events one can grasp and conceptualize a structure of the effective powers" (Horkheimer, 1932:1). This theory would be based on the results of historical studies and the individual sciences and would therefore strive for the status of "science" (ibid: 1 and 4). Yet, these investigations would not exclude philosophy, "for it is not affiliation to a specific discipline but its importance for the theory of society which determines the choice of material" (ibid:1). (Kellner, 2010, p. 5).

Although the Institute's earlier work was situated in the Marxist tradition, under Horkheimer it began to move away from orthodox Marxism to focus more on

> a program of supradisciplinary research, which would investigate current social and political problems. This project would unite "philosophers, sociologists, economists, historians, and psychologists in an ongoing research community who would do together what in other disciplines one individual does alone in the laboratory,—which is what genuine scientists have always done: namely, to pursue the great philosophical questions using the most refined scientific methods; to reformulate and to make more precise the questions in the course of work as demanded by the object; and to develop new methods without losing sight of the universal" (ibid:41). (Kellner, 2010, pp. 3–4)

The rise of Fascism and Nazism in Europe led some of the founders of the Institute, including Horkheimer, to flee to the United States. After World War II, Horkheimer and other members returned to Frankfurt to continue their work. However, in the 1950s and 1960s the Institute became the subject of criticism from Marxist groups, who claimed that it was watering down scientific principles and Marxism, and compromising revolutionary ideas.

Despite these criticisms, Critical Social Theory has evolved, and its applications in education as Critical Pedagogy; in feminist studies as Critical Feminist Theory; in studies of race, gender, and ethnic studies, as Critical Race Theory are evident. According to Fay (1987), cited in Freeman and Vasconcelos (2010), all branches of Critical Social Theory share four tenets, namely (a) a theory of false consciousness, which explains the nature and process through which social members' values and beliefs become obscured and distorted by dominant ideologies; (b) a theory of crisis, which locates and describes the source and nature of the oppression in question; (c) a theory of education, which accounts for the conditions and processes necessary for the enlightenment or alternative visions to the surface, and (d) a theory of transformative action, which details the kinds of actions and alterations needed to resolve the identified crisis. (p. 12)

A theory of false consciousness holds that people who suffer from oppression sometimes internalize the values and beliefs of their oppressors and participate in maintaining their own oppression. To change their situation, they must be reeducated or must reeducate themselves. However, this reeducation process is not a simple process, and it must not be confused with ignorance. Both the oppressed and oppressor could be victims of false consciousness. Referring to Freire's (1970/1993) *Pedagogy of the Oppressed*, Freeman and Vasconcelos (2010) noted that the road to addressing the false consciousness problem lies in both the teacher-student, doctor-patient, or staff-client understanding their "interdependent, often unintended, contribution to the maintenance of the oppressive situation" (p. 12).

A theory of crisis holds that not all crises are real; that some crises are manufactured and are designed to perpetuate the dependence and domination of the oppressed. For example,

> Crises such as the "achievement gap" or welfare mothers contribute to maintaining a system in which people who are so identified are seen as problems in relation to people who are not, rather than considering that a system that contributes to these effects is in need of reconfiguration (Freeman & Vasconcelos, 2010, p. 14).

A theory of education holds that in an oppressive or unjust society, education must be for liberation and not to perpetuate the status quo. Such an education must be based on "dialogue" and "problem posing" (Freire, 1970/1993). However, it should not be dogmatic and utopian; rather it should be based on real issues, and should lead to self-discovery and the development of independent, critical thinking beings capable of taking charge of their own destinies.

A theory of transformative action holds that the logical step from being conscious of one's own oppression and its causes is to take positive action to change the situation. However, we must distinguish between individual action and social action, and the role they play in the transformative process.

The above four tenets of Critical Social Theory provide us with a framework for critiquing social formations and relationships. As Freeman and Vasconcelos (2010) reminded us:

> Critical theory offers a theoretical lens for assessing the relationships individuals have with the social structures and institutional practices they work within and encounter every day. It offers a way to understand better the effects these social structures have on people's beliefs, ideologies, actions, interpretations, and communicative practices, while also generating insight into the processes that resist, challenge, or reshape dominant forms of thinking and acting. (p. 17)

Critical race theory

Critical Race Theory (CRT) is a theory that postulates that race and racism are central to understanding social relations, economic inequalities, and political oppression in American society. It seeks not only to understand the causes and consequences of a social phenomenon, but also to transform it through the production of a new, emancipatory praxis. The historical context of Critical Race Theory was best summed up by Hatch (2007) in the following words:

> In defining critical race theory, it is important to make a distinction between the deep historical tradition of critical theorizing about race and racism and a specific body of American legal scholarship that emerged in the 1970s and 1980s in response to the successes and failures of the Civil Rights Movement struggles for the freedom and liberation of people of color of the 1950s and 1960s. While this new school of legal thought coined the phrase "critical race theory" to signal a new critical analysis of the role of the law in propagating and maintaining racism, this movement is part of a broader intellectual tradition of critical theories of race and anti-racist struggle that has political roots in the work of pioneering scholar-activists like Frederick Douglass, Ida Wells-Barnett, and W. E. B. Du Bois. Using this broader framework, critical race theory can be viewed as a diagnostic body of "intellectual activism" scholarship that seeks to identify the pressure points for anti-racist struggle. (p. 1)

Although there are several scholars (Delgado, Matsuda, Crenshaw, Tate, Ladson-Billings, and Collins) who made great contributions to the development of CRT, to understand CRT, one must appreciate the contributions of Derrick Bell (1930–2011). Derrick Bell was the first tenured African American Professor of Law at Harvard University and the author of many books including, *Race, Racism, and American Law*; *Faces at the Bottom of the Well*; and *Silent Covenants*, to name a few. According to Guinier and Torres (2011),

> Indeed, Bell was one of the pioneers of critical race theory, which challenged liberalism for failing to go far enough in opposing the entrenched interests that historically benefited from the racial caste system that was being dismantled. According to criti-

cal race theory, the defining elements of postwar racial liberalism were its pragmatic devotion to a single strategy of litigation, its static view of American racism, and its focus on top-down social reform, which emphasized the corrosive effect of individual prejudice and the importance of interracial contact in promoting tolerance. As Bell recognized, that strategy left poor whites haunted by the sense that they had been betrayed by the elites; at the same time, it enabled them to blame blacks as the beneficiaries of that betrayal. As an early proponent of the theory, Bell freed scholars from an old fashioned reliance on fixed racial categories and introduced the idea that "race" was a verb, not just a noun. Thus, people are "raced" by the larger society rather than simply by their genetic makeup. (p. 2)

Jones (2002) noted that Bell is a "crucial figure for understanding the development of critical race theory from the 1970s through the 1990s" (p. 32). While at Harvard, he taught civil rights law and served as a mentor to many students of color. One of the courses Bell taught at Harvard was titled, "Race, Racism and American Law" (Jones, 2002). In this course, Bell drew heavily on his past experience as a civil rights lawyer with the NAACP Legal Defense Fund in the 1950s and 1960s. He used his classes as a laboratory to test ideas about civil rights law, and focused his efforts on preparing activist lawyers who would not only know and interpret the law, but would also be activists in their communities. However, soon it became clear to him that after all these years, the gains of the civil rights era were being eroded, and that "The law never solved anything—attempts to go beyond symbolism were fruitless. Racism always played a major role in the fate of African Americans under the law" (Jones, 2002, p. 35).

Through his research and teaching, Derrick Bell discovered that the courts consistently have not paid attention to the role of race in deciding important cases that impacted the lives of African Americans. Instead, they have relied on traditional interpretation of the law. The Supreme Court, he noted,

was far more ready to invalidate overtly discriminatory policies that ended indefensible restrictions on the rights of Blacks than it is willing to tackle the more subtle rules that do not create blatant classifications, but in their racist administration are as pernicious as the most flagrant Jim Crow signs. (Jones, 2002, p. 37)

Derrick Bell also found that in all the major Supreme Court cases (e.g., *Plessy v. Ferguson* and *Brown v. Board of Education*), the decisions that the Court took were based on what he called "interest convergence," meaning that the interest of Blacks in achieving racial equality was accommodated only because it converged with the interest of Whites (Jones, 2002, p. 39). The Supreme Court made calculated decisions in favor of Blacks only because the interests of Whites were not threatened or undermined. The Court saw in these cases opportunities to end official, court-sanctioned segregation, in order to demonstrate to Blacks and the world that America was determined to end racial inequality, but at the same time send a signal to Whites that it was business as usual, because there were no enforceable remedies. This history of civil rights cases, particularly those related to school desegregation and affirmative action, showed consistent patterns of interest convergence. This prompted Bell to critique the strategies used by civil rights lawyers, and to question whether they were too formal and not realistic. He advocated for a "racial realism" that is based on pragmatism and on the interests of the clients. He criticized civil right lawyers for using a model of litigation that was too bureaucratic and that often ignored the client's interest in favor of enforcement of desegregation at all cost. He noticed that prior to desegregation African Americans were forced to set up and run their own education infrastructure that included schools, teachers, principals, and support staff. Although segregation deprived them of financial support and resources, they had control over the education of their children. In retrospect, Bell lamented that "the effort to enforce the all deliberate speed provisions of Brown only resulted in a decade of litigation with little progress. Instead, the Courts could have ordered the immediate and total equalization of school facilities and resources" (Jones, 2002, p. 43).

His experiences with the NAACP Legal Defense Fund, teaching at Harvard, the challenge of taking on civil rights cases on school desegregation and affirmative action, and the issue of interest convergence, all led Derrick Bell and his colleagues to propose a theory of American legal studies that puts race and racism front and center. This theory they called Critical Race Theory. To operationalize this theory, they drew upon a popular, African sociocultural tradition of storytelling. Storytelling uses counternarratives to argue for civil rights and social and economic justice for African Americans. According to Yasso (2005), "initially CRT scholarship focused its critique on the slow pace and unrealized promise of the Civil Rights legislation. As a result, many of the critiques launched were articulated in Black vs. White terms. Women and People of Color who felt their gendered, classed, sexual, immigrant and language experiences and histories were being silenced, challenged this tendency towards the Black/White binary" (p. 72). As a result of this internal contradiction and struggles within the CRT community, the movement has been transformed, and today it includes "racialized experiences of women, Latinas/os, Native Americans and Asian Americans" (Yasso, 2005, p. 72).

Core theme in critical race theory

Hatch (2007) identified five core themes in CRT. The first one deals with race and racism. From a CRT point of view, race is a social construction that is a by-product of a particular type of social interaction, relationship, and organization. Racism is an instrument of domination, exploitation, and dehumanization. Race and racism are prevalent in American and other economically advanced societies despite the growing misconception that we are living in a postracial society.

The second theme holds that racism not only exists at the individual level, but also at the institutional level. Institutions set up structures that discriminate and/or disadvantage certain groups based on their race, gender, sexual orientation, and nationality. Critical race theorists understand that institutional racism poses the greatest challenge in the fight for social justice, and that just as individuals who exhibit racist tendencies must be held accountable, so must institutions that practiced racism.

The third theme is "that critical race theory has traditionally used and continues to represent an interdisciplinary approach to the study of race and racism" (Hatch, 2007, p. 2). This means that Critical Race Theory draws from and is enriched by a diverse group of stakeholders, disciplines, philosophies, ideologies, epistemologies, and research methodologies. It is this intellectual capital and diversity that makes Critical Race Theory a powerful framework for critiquing oppression, injustice, and discrimination.

The fourth theme concerns the methodological dexterity of Critical Race Theory. As a result of a diverse group of stakeholders who represent different disciplines with a common interest, critical race theorists enjoyed "methodological pluralism," unlike other scholars and/or activists. The implication is that understanding the different research methodologies, what they are capable of achieving, and their limitations is critical to the training and practice of critical race theorists.

The fifth and final theme proposed by Hatch (2007) deals with the relationship between science and race, and racism. The history of science is littered with false or erroneous claims about African Americans, women, and People of Color that are based on junk science and have had devastating consequences. Critical Race Theory "has long contested these claims that upheld racial hierarchies and justified ideologies of White supremacy" (Hatch, 2007, p. 2).

Our interpretation and discussion of the data on the academic and professional journeys of African American women scientists will be guided by the core principles of CRT. However, we will focus specifically on the following:

1. That race is a determining factor in the academic and professional lives of African American women scientists,
2. That gender is a determining factor for women's success in science, and
3. That access to and ownership of resources are critical to the success of African American women scientists in science and science careers.

There is well-documented evidence to support the first principle (Jones et al., 2007; Bell, 2004; Norman et al., 2001; Atwater, 2000; Ladson-Billings and Tate, 1995; Collins, 1991). In addition, there are vital statistics on the state of science in the United States, including numbers of women, minorities, and persons with disabilities from the National Science Foundation (National Science Foundation (NSF), 2004a, 2004b, 2007, 2011) and other government scientific agencies that provide ample evidence to support the second principle. Science is a resource-intensive profession where those with access to and ownership of the means of producing science succeed, and those without often do not succeed in science and science careers; hence there are few poor and traditionally disadvantaged groups represented in science and science careers. In Chapters 9 and 10, we will use our modified version of CRT as a framework to interpret our data on the academic and professional journeys of African American women scientists. We will use the strategies of "storytelling" practiced by Bell and other CRT scholars (Delgado and Stefancic, 2001) to represent the diverse voices of African American women scientists and their stories of resilience and success.

CHAPTER 7
Survey and Case Study Methodology

The survey

In preparing this book we drew from three methodological traditions, namely survey research, case study, and research synthesis. This chapter gives an explanation of the methodology used. The first step was to conduct a sample survey of African American women scientists with a view to answering the following questions: What are the personal characteristics and academic backgrounds of African American women scientists? What led them to careers in science? What academic trajectories did they follow? What professional trajectories did they follow? What factors contributed to their success in science? This chapter focuses on the analysis of the survey data.

The sampling plan was to develop a sampling frame by enlisting the assistance of Historically Black Colleges and Universities (HBCU), national Black scientific associations, national Black women's associations, the Association for Women in Science, the American Association of University Women, the American Association for the Advancement of Science, and other professional organizations. Between 200 and 500 scientists were to be sampled using stratified random sampling techniques (Czaja and Blair, 1996) to ensure representation by scientific discipline, professional affiliation, and region of the country.

Unfortunately, this plan was not viable because of time, resources, and legal constraints involved in obtaining a sampling frame. The following alternative sampling strategy was adopted. The survey instrument was sent to representatives from the National Society of Black Engineers (NSBE) and the National Society of Black Physicists (NSBP) who agreed to distribute the survey to their female members and affiliates. Respondents from NSBE and NSBP were encouraged to forward the survey to their colleagues. Using word of mouth, e-mail, conferences, and professional networks, other participants were recruited. In addition, a research assistant was hired to mine HBCU websites for e-mail addresses of African American women science faculty and researchers. The survey instrument, an abstract of the research, and an informed consent form were sent to over 100 participants via e-mail and regular USPS mail. The total number of participants who received the survey is estimated to be between 150 and 200. An exact number was not possible to determine because the professional societies cited privacy issues and only agreed to send the survey on our behalf.

Instruments

Although a number of survey instruments have been developed to collect data on gender differences in STEM careers (Horning, 2003; Kang, 2003; Matyas, 1991; National Research Council, 1981; National Science Foundation (NSF), 1990; Rapoport, 2004; Sonnert and Holton, 1995; Yentsch & Sindermann, 1992), surveys specifically devoted to academic and professional trajectories of African American women scientists are hard to come by, and are, at best, nonexistent. Consequently, in this study, it was necessary to develop a new instrument that would meet the needs of the study.

The development of the survey instrument was informed by the above-mentioned studies and/or reports, our own experiences with colleagues and friends who are African American women scientists and/or pursuing science education, and our prior knowledge and experience of the research topic. Specifically, the survey instruments consisted of 19 items grouped into the following categories: personal history, academic background, and professional trajectories (see Appendix I). The professional trajectories category included open-ended items, which focused on factors that contributed to success as well as challenges in pursuing a career in science. In addition, this category included two rating-scale items that asked participants about their experiences with race and gender discrimination. Prior to the implementation of the study, the instrument was peer-reviewed by a microbiologist, a literacy specialist, a psychologist, and a teacher educator, all of whom were women and African American.

Data collection and analysis

Most of the survey instruments were returned electronically. However, a few respondents returned their survey via fax and USPS mail. Although the survey was sent to between 150 and 200 participants, only 38 surveys were returned. To improve response rate, follow-up e-mails were sent and phone calls made, but this did not lead to any improvement in participants' responses.

The analysis procedure consisted of two steps. First, the rating-scale responses were entered into a database. To determine if there were any discrepancies between the database and the completed surveys (raw data), one-third of the completed surveys were randomly selected and cross-referenced with the database. No recording errors or discrepancies were found. The data were then summarized using descriptive statistics and frequency distribution charts. The analysis of rating-scale responses was conducted using JMP Statistical Discovery Software (SAS Institute, 2002).

Second, the open-ended responses were converted into a Microsoft Word file and read multiple times. Using the inductive approach to qualitative research (Thomas, 2006), the data were sorted into themes using the cut-and-paste function. To test the validity of these themes, we sent the Word files to two of our colleagues and asked them to categorize the responses. Their categories were consistent with our original themes. Each theme was discussed with reference to the specific research question to which it was related.

Although the survey yielded valuable information and provided insight into the study questions, it was limited in terms of its response rate. One of the most important methodological issues in survey research is sampling. The type of sampling used in a survey will determine, to a large extent, the type of inferences that can be made. Having a sample that is representative and randomly selected is more valuable, because it allows the researcher to generalize findings to the population being studied. As indicated earlier, the original sampling plan met with unexpected resource, legal, and time challenges. At the time of adopting an alternative strategy, the time allocated for the study was running out and there were no additional resources. Survey research offers a broad brushstroke of information that can be generalized to the target population, but to enrich our data we also conducted a case study which allowed us to drill in-depth regarding the professional journeys of African American women scientists.

There is no doubt that the subject matter this book addresses is a challenging one. Several studies (Adenika-Marrow, 1996; Clewell and Ginorio, 2002; Gregory, 2001; Hanson, 2006; Thomas and Hollenshead, 2001) have confirmed that African American women scientists and women scientists of color in general experience gender and race bias in academic science. Historically, the issue of race in the US is very controversial, and most scholars and/or researchers prefer to leave it alone or to pretend that it does not exist. Studying the interaction of race and gender in science is therefore not easy, and requires discipline, patience, and persistence.

Case study

According to Robert Stake (2010),

> Two realities exist simultaneously and separately within every human activity. One is the reality of personal experience, and one is the reality of group and societal

relationship. The two realities connect, they overlap, they merge, but they are recognizably different. (p. 18)

To study how things work, he suggested that researchers use different research strategies for different realities. For instance, in our case, a survey research strategy was chosen to understand the "generalities" of a particular group (African American women scientists). However, that strategy only took us so far, and we needed another strategy to develop an understanding of the "particularities" (personal experiences of African American women scientists).

To strengthen and improve the original study, we purposefully selected a subsample from the pool of respondents, and conducted a case study. We sent out a call to participate via e-mail and by word of mouth to all who responded to the survey. We received responses from seven African American women scientists who agreed to participate in the case study. The guiding questions for the case study were a modified version of the survey. A semistructured interview guide was developed to collect interview data (see Appendix II). The guide consisted of 12 open-ended questions that focused on the following variables: academic preparation, professional experience, family background, parental involvement, disposition toward science, challenges in pursuing science, and success factors. The interviews were conducted over the phone and varied from 45 minutes to one hour in duration. All the interviews were audiotaped and transcribed. Each participant scientist was sent a copy of her transcript for review and feedback.

The interview data were analyzed using a two-step analytical process. Firstly, the data were read and open-coded (Strauss and Corbin, 1990) independently by the two authors. Codes and the coding processes were discussed before the final codes were mutually agreed upon. The mutually agreed-upon codes were then used to recode the interviews. The coded interview data were organized into themes using the seven variables of interest mentioned above. Secondly, a question-by-candidate matrix was developed. This matrix was used to aggregate the data, examine them from a "big picture" perspective, and identify patterns. Because our main aim in conducting the case study was to gain an in-depth understanding of the academic and professional journeys of African American women scientists, our interpretation and discussion of the data were guided by the framework of Critical Race Theory, as discussed in the previous chapter. Within the data, we looked for confirmation or a lack of confirmation of the three CRT principles discussed in Chapter 6. Based on our interpretation, we developed a narrative that captures the stories about the academic and professional trajectory of each participant scientist.

Research synthesis can be used as a stand-alone research strategy, or it can be used to address specific, methodological needs in a specific study. In preparing this book, we felt it necessary to employ research synthesis to enable us to search, identify, review, and synthesize past and present studies in the field of gender and science that would inform and enhance our work. We borrowed from recent studies in science education and program evaluation (Coryn, Noakes, Westine, and Schroter, 2011; Minner, Levy, and Century, 2010; Sadler, Burgin, McKinney, and Ponjuan, 2010) that serve as models for conducting robust research synthesis. The contents of this book were produced using a combination of survey research, case study, and the research synthesis described above. The chapters which follow give an analysis of the data from the survey and case study.

CHAPTER 8

Survey Findings

This chapter focuses on the outcomes of the survey research. The guiding research questions were used to organize and present the findings from the survey. The lens of Critical Race Theory is used throughout as a tool for interpretation and discussion.

What are the personal characteristics and academic backgrounds of African American women scientists?

Figure 8.1 shows the age group of African American women scientists who responded to the survey. As can be seen, 68 percent of respondents were up to 35 years of age, 18 percent were between 35 and 45 years, and 8 percent were between 45 and 55. Only two respondents were between 55 and 75 years old. With regard to their marital status, 79 percent of the respondents were single or unmarried, and 10.5 percent were married (see Figure 8.2).

Figure 8.1. Age Group of African American Women Scientist Respondents

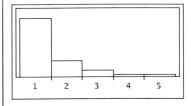

Age group	Count	%
1 = 0–35	26	68
2 = 35–45	7	18
3 = 45–55	3	8
4 = 55–65	1	3
5 = 65–75	1	3
6 = >75	0	
Total	38	

Figure 8.2. Marital Status of African American Women Scientist Respondents

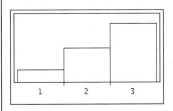

M_Status	Count	%
1 = Married	4	10.5
2 = Unmarried	11	29
3 = Single	19	50
N Missing	4	10.5
Total	38	

What led them to careers in science?

Except for one, all participants responded to this survey question. Participants' responses can be categorized into the following themes: love of mathematics and science, teacher and/or counselor support, and the nature of science. A majority of the participants' responses fell under the theme, "love of mathematics and science." This theme includes all responses in which participants indicated that their love for mathematics and science at an early age was what led them to careers in science. Examples of responses that captured this theme are as follows:

I loved math and chemistry.

Math and science were my favorite subjects through elementary and high schools.

I enjoyed math and science; I participated in high school programs that introduced students to science and math.

I liked math. I also liked tinkering with electrical household objects.

A love for science.

I always enjoyed math and science since grade school and also by being involved in . . . high school program.

Science is the only subject I liked in school.

I was very good in math and science growing up, so I decided to go into a field that utilized my math and science skills.

I have always excelled in math and science throughout my educational path. I wanted to explore a career that had both challenges and allowed creativity.

Love of chemistry.

In high school, I had a strong skill set in math and science and I liked it, so naturally I pursued a degree in engineering.

I was interested in the subject matter since 4th grade when we had science fairs.

I fell in love with geology, and though I was originally into liberal arts, I decided to go for it.

Although love of mathematics may not necessarily lead to success in mathematics, it is an important ingredient in the "success in science" equation, hence, according to Davis (1995), "Mathematics is an important tool in the practice of science and, without math course work, students are filtered out of scientific and technological careers" (p. 193). The above finding also demonstrates the importance of a positive disposition toward science at an early age, and echoes similar findings by Hanson (2006). Using National Educational Longitude Survey (NELS) data, Hanson examined issues of access, achievement, and attitudes toward science of a subsample of 581 young African American and 3,365 White women taken from a nationally representative sample of 24,599 eighth graders. Participants were interviewed at four intervals: when they were in the tenth grade, when they were seniors, when they completed high school, and when they were about twenty-five years old. According to Hanson (2006),

> The examination of young African American science experience from eighth grade through early adult years (twelve years later) in three aspects of science (access, achievement and attitudes) revealed considerable interest in and access to science by young African American women. However, it is in attitudes, even more than access that young African American women distinguish themselves. Starting in eighth grade and continuing into early adult years, young African American women are often more positive about science than their white counterparts. (p. 136)

Perhaps these young women are not as susceptible to the double issues of gender and race in science, yet. This explains their positive disposition and love of math and science. However, Ladson-Billings and Tate (1995) warned,

> Issues of gender bias also figure in inequitable schooling. Females receive less attention from teachers, are counseled away from or out of advanced mathematics and science courses, and although they receive better grades than their male counterparts, their grades do not translate into advantages in college admission and/or the workplace. (p. 31)

As will be seen in the following chapter, another factor for these women is family support. Today's parents understand that they must be advocates for their children. Historically, this family or parental support has been part and parcel of education for African Americans. During the 1900s, most Blacks were barred from participating in White institutions and organizations. However, Selena Sloan Butler, a teacher and wife of a physician in Atlanta, had followed the development of the National Congress of Parents and Teachers (NCPT) in 1910. An association called the Colored Parent Teacher Association was established to represent the needs of African American parents. This organization was barred from meeting jointly with the White NCPT, not by NCPT bylaws, but by state laws. It was not until 1960 that the two organizations met jointly and formed a coalition (Herzog, 1997). This institutional racism may have served to keep African Americans and Whites separate, but instead the result was a determination by African American parents to advocate for their children. This age-old determination may have played a key role in the support and passion the respondents to our survey expressed that they received and held as young children and adolescents. The comments below also highlight the importance of family and community support.

Support from teachers and counselors was the second most frequent reason given by respondents for going into science. However, this was often made with reference to family and community involvement. For instance:

> *I was influenced by my science teacher, the family and the community. Science experiments done at all levels of my education.*

> *My counselor in high school suggested that I should become an engineer because I had excellent grades in science and mathematics and my standardized testing scores were always the highest.*

> *At an early age, teachers have encouraged my involvement in science. Throughout middle school and high school, teachers and counselors have enrolled me in science and math summer camps.*

> *Encouragement from high school teachers and friends in the community/church.*

> *Convinced by high school teachers/guidance counselor because I was "good in math & science."*

> *My high school science teacher.*

Nature of science (NOS) "is the sum total of the 'rules of the game' leading to knowledge production and the evaluation of truth claims in the natural sciences" (McComas, 2004). In this study the theme, NOS, is used to describe the interest and challenges that science as a field of study generates, which act as a source of attraction for young scientists. Some of the respondents indicated that they were attracted to science careers because they found science interesting and challenging, as evident in the following statements.

> *I like the way science and technology challenges me.*

> *There is so much to learn in the study of science. Never-ending and continually evolving.*

> *My father was a veterinarian and I always remembered sitting in his lab and looking through microscopes at cells. I found it fascinating.*

> *Interest in science, their underlying principles.*

> *I have always had a passion for computer science and how things work.*

Interest in science as a child.

Personal Interest.

Interest in science from an early age; targeted experiences (e.g., field trips, college visits) during AP biology class in high school.

I found science challenging and interesting.

What academic trajectories did they follow?

The findings from the survey indicated that the majority of African American women scientists who responded attended public schools (66 percent), while 16 percent attended private schools (see Figure 8.3). It is important to note that the category, "Others," refers to respondents who attended more than one type of school (for instance, public and private, or public and parochial). Among respondents, about 45 percent earned BS degrees, 18 percent earned MS degrees, and 31 percent earned PhDs (see Figure 8.4). Data on science and engineering degree recipients by race and/or ethnicity collected by NSF showed that in 2001, the recipients of 10.2 percent of bachelor's degrees, 7.3 percent of master's degrees, and 4.0 percent of doctorates were Black women (Hill and Johnson, 2004).

Because of the small sample size, this survey is unable to provide information on the representation of African American women scientists in the different science disciplines. Figure 8.5 indicates that 55 percent of the respondents are affiliated with the field of engineering, 10 percent are in the biological sciences, and the rest represent chemistry, environmental sciences, health sciences, and microbiology. A survey of employed science and engineering doctorate holders in 2001 showed that there were 34,660 computer and information scientists and 80 were Black women. The discipline of life sciences (i.e., agricultural, biological, medical, and environmental) had 107,850 scientists, 770 of whom were Black women. There were 21,900 mathematical scientists, 200 of whom were Black women; 73,840 physical and related scientists, 180 of whom were Black women; and 75,420 engineers, 140 of whom were Black women (NSF, 2001).

What professional trajectories did they follow?

From this survey, it is clear that most of the respondents are employed in government and industry (see Figure 8.6). In addition, 47 percent reported less than 5 years of work experience, while 29 percent have between 10–15 years work experience (see Figure 8.7). Figure 8.8 shows that the primary

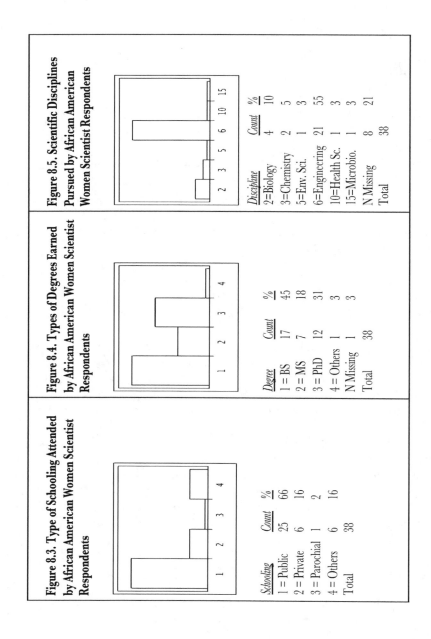

Figure 8.3. Type of Schooling Attended by African American Women Scientist Respondents

Schooling	Count	%
1 = Public	25	66
2 = Private	6	16
3 = Parochial	1	2
4 = Others	6	16
Total	38	

Figure 8.4. Types of Degrees Earned by African American Women Scientist Respondents

Degree	Count	%
1 = BS	17	45
2 = MS	7	18
3 = PhD	12	31
4 = Others	1	3
N Missing	1	3
Total	38	

Figure 8.5. Scientific Disciplines Pursued by African American Women Scientist Respondents

Discipline	Count	%
2=Biology	4	10
3=Chemistry	2	5
5=Env. Sci.	1	3
6=Engineering	21	55
10=Health Sc.	1	3
15=Microbio.	1	3
N Missing	8	21
Total	38	

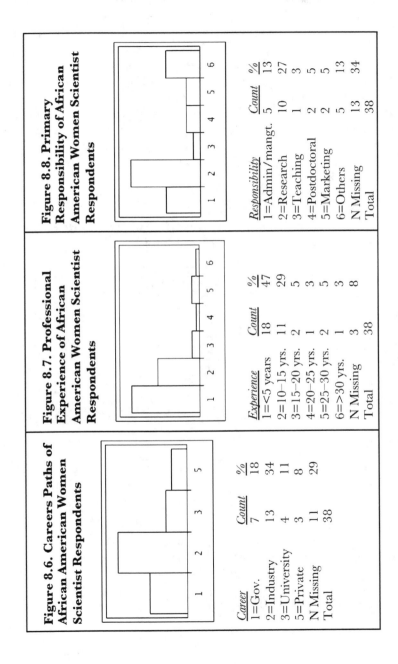

Figure 8.6. Careers Paths of African American Women Scientist Respondents

Career	Count	%
1=Gov.	7	18
2=Industry	13	34
3=University	4	11
5=Private	3	8
N Missing	11	29
Total	38	

Figure 8.7. Professional Experience of African American Women Scientist Respondents

Experience	Count	%
1=<5 years	18	47
2=10–15 yrs.	11	29
3=15–20 yrs.	2	5
4=20–25 yrs.	1	3
5=25–30 yrs.	2	5
6=>30 yrs.	1	3
N Missing	3	8
Total	38	

Figure 8.8. Primary Responsibility of African American Women Scientist Respondents

Responsibility	Count	%
1=Admin/mangt.	5	13
2=Research	10	27
3=Teaching	1	3
4=Postdoctoral	2	5
5=Marketing	2	5
6=Others	5	13
N Missing	13	34
Total	38	

responsibility of respondents is in research (26 percent) and administration and/or management (13 percent). The category "Others" accounts for 13 percent of primary responsibility. It is interesting to note that teaching is reported as one of the least responsibilities of respondents. In the late 1800s and early 1900s, education was the field into which most African American women were funneled. Unlike Figure 8.6 and Figure 8.8, Figure 8.9 paints a different picture. In Figure 8.9, the percentage of science and engineering doctorate recipients by employment sector is displayed graphically as a way to compare the sample in this survey to a nationally representative sample of scientists and engineers. The data, which were obtained from the NSF website (NSF, 2009), show the percentage of women scientists and engineers employed in various sectors in 2006.

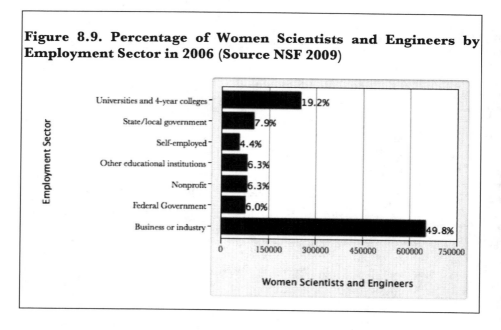

Figure 8.9. Percentage of Women Scientists and Engineers by Employment Sector in 2006 (Source NSF 2009)

As can be seen, four-year colleges and/or universities and business or industry account for most of the employment of women scientists and engineers. Whether this is true for the population of African American women scientists remains to be investigated. According to the National Academy of Sciences (2007),

Academe is purportedly a meritocracy that rewards objectively determined accomplishment. However, many studies document that both bias and structural barriers built into academic institutions and the occupation of professor limit many women's ability to be hired and promoted in university faculties. In fact, the academy has perpetuated patterns of bias that devalue women and minorities and their abilities, aspirations, accomplishments, and roles. (p. 215)

Bleier's (1988) findings support the idea that academia has duplicated and repeated the bias that existed in a male-dominated field since the early 1870s. If this is the case for women in general, then it has a major impact on African American women specifically.

What factors contributed to their success in science?

The factors that contributed to success in science vary greatly. However, according to Sonnert and Holton (1995), success in science is a function of the following factors: choice of institution, choice of research topics and field, publications of research results, mentors, the political game, networking, and hard work. For women, the researchers noted the following factors: balancing career, balancing marriage and motherhood, the ability to handle discrimination, and the ability to deal with positive and negative feedback in a timely and appropriate manner, are critical to success in science. Barres (2006) put the onus of responsibility on the institution, and cited four other factors that included

1. Enhancing leadership diversity in academic and scientific institutions;

2. Making sure there are diverse faculty role models, and running fair job searches;
3. Academic leadership and women must speak out in the face of discrimination so that it cannot be swept under the carpet; and
4. Make competitive selection processes for grants and other resources more fair.

Findings from this study show that African American women scientists' success in science is attributed to two major factors, which in this study will be called the *contextual* and *environmental factors*. Contextual factors contributing to success can be defined as self-determination, family support, and religious faith. Environmental factors refer to a work environment with supportive supervisors and mentors. When asked to identify factors that contributed to their success in science, African American women scientists responded in the following voices:

Being proactive, exceeding expectations by doing literature searches to determine the basis behind the work being done and the techniques used.

Determination.

My success as a scientist in the work place can be attributed to several factors. I was qualified and confident in my ability. I had learned to do with less, and I am able to wait to get what I wanted or to accomplish a goal. My environment was also a factor. There were several people who cared enough to keep you on task.

My determination, family reliance on me, and my thirst to learn new and challenging things that is going to help me when I start my business.
My faith in God and my willingness to want to succeed and do my best in all my endeavors.

A positive and never giving up attitude.

My drive and determination and mentors.

Desire to do a good job.

Once again, discipline has played a major factor. Working for a small, private-owned . . . company, I have had to rely on self-determination and motivation to prove myself professionally. Just knowing that even with a science degree from one of the top engineering schools in the country I won't automatically be recognized as knowledgeable in my field has prevented me from having early hurdles brought on by complacency. I've known from day one on my job that having the degree is not enough and that I have to prove I earned the degree because of what I know.

My ability to work well with others, as well as problem-solve and come up with new ideas.

As an engineer in the work place, I think that I am successful because I am resourceful. I know how to ask questions when I don't understand something and often engineers will not be resourceful and open up to others for help.

More than anything it's persistence, not willing to accept poorly engineered parts or systems.

God.

Support and encouragement from family.

The Grace of God, Jesus Christ.

Faith in God, family support, self-confidence, ability to deal with isolation.

Enthusiasm, volunteer for every task or job, research job, submit work on time or let someone know I need help.

Doing more than what is required.

Dedication, desire to improve the quality of life for people.

The voices of these women above offer a window on how they navigate a system that assumes that they are less than their peers. Their responses show that both environmental and contextual factors play major roles in thriving in scientific fields. They have learned, through the legacy of struggle (Collins, 1991), that they have to do more than expected; be determined; not expect acknowledgment; do more with less; and maintain their belief in God, family, and community. This legacy has empowered them to develop a type of consciousness and a sense of resistance that allow them to move beyond just managing, to being persistent, dedicated, and conscious of the challenges in the environment in which they work.

The role that work environment plays in success in academic science has been well documented by Settles et al. (2006), Bystydzienski and Bird (2006), Ferber (2003), and Horning (2003). Respondents in this study indicated that having a nurturing work environment, which includes supportive mentors and supervisors, contributed to their success in science. Most of the respondents did not identify one element of the work environment, but rather a combination of supportive mentor, supervisor, and workplace. Examples of responses are as follows:

. . . supportive management.

Supportive mentors.

Self-confidence, supportive colleagues, positive work environment.

. . . having supervisor that acted as my mentor.

Direction and motivation from professors and other faculty members; good internship experiences.

Supportive leadership and co-workers.

Hard work, good mentors (I would have more but I've only been working for 4 months).

Supportive, balanced and nurturing supervisors.

Great mentors and lab mates.

The above findings are consistent with the earlier findings in Barres (2006), West and Curtis (2006), National Academy of Sciences (2007), and others. Besides the above findings, other responses related to the training that participants received. For instance,

My training at college about academic and corporate America.

The training and research acquired from the University of . . . has equipped me with innovative and investigative skills.

God, hard work, graduate training, and support from family.

Race and gender discrimination, and equal treatment in the workplace

Although unequal treatment and discrimination by race, gender, nationality, religion, and sexual orientation is prohibited under the U.S. constitution, it still exists in the workplace. Critical race theorists use the term *institutional racism* to identify this type of discrimination. Hatch (2007) explained this as follows:

> An organizing theme of critical race theory is that there is not, and has never been, one monolithic and universal form of racism.
>
> In 1967, black radicals Stokely Carmichael and Charles V. Hamilton coined the term "institutional racism" to identify how racism is embedded in social structures and multiple institutions. . . . Drawing on these formulations, contemporary critical race theories understand racism as a vast and complicated system of institutionalized practices that structure the allocation of social, economic, and political power in unjust and racially coded ways. (p. 5)

The workplace is one of these social structures. In this study, African American women scientists were asked to respond to two related, but different statements about discrimination in the workplace and equal treatment in the work place. With regard to the statement, "As an African American woman scientist, I have experienced race and gender discrimination in the workplace," about 70 percent of the respondents agreed or strongly agreed (see Figure 8.10). When asked to respond to the statement, "As an African American woman scientist, I am treated equally to my other colleagues in the workplace," 68 percent of the respondents strongly disagreed or disagreed, while 32 percent agreed or strongly agreed (see Figure 8.11). These findings confirmed earlier ones (Thomas and Hollenshead, 2001), and suggest that more work needs to be done to tackle the problem of race relations, not only in the STEM workplace, but also in society as a whole. Hatch (2007) described Critical Race Theory as grounded in the lived experiences and voices of subordinated communities. As these comments show, the participants speak from their lived experiences, and in Chapter 10, these same themes can be seen.

The United States has enacted major laws against discrimination, for instance, Title VII of the Civil Rights Act of 1964, Title IX in 1972, the Science and Engineering Equal Opportunity Act of 1980, to name a few.

These laws were enacted to prevent discrimination based on race, color, religion, sex, and national origin. What the evidence in the survey findings indicates is that discrimination is a major issue for the success of African American women in science. This validates the position of Ladson-Billings and Tate (1995) that race continues to be a major factor in terms of inequity in the US.

The history of women in science highlights the process whereby gender determined the role women would play in this field. This survey points to how this is still an issue. For African American women, the issue of gender is added to the issue of their race, so that there is a double impediment in terms of their struggle for equity in the field of science. The history of African American women in science cannot be separated from the history of African Americans overall in the US. With all of the progress that has been made, race still plays a major role. W. E. B. Du Bois (1903), a century earlier, said it best when he stated that, "the problem of the Twentith Century is the problem of the color line" (p. 1).

Figure 8.10. Experienced Race and Gender Discrimination in the Workplace.

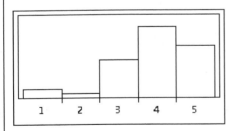

Race/gender discrimination	Count	%
1=No opinion	2	5
2=Strongly disagree	1	3
3=Disagree	8	22
4=Agree	15	40
5=Strongly agree	11	30
Total	37	

Figure 8.11. Treated Equally to My Other Colleagues in the Workplace.

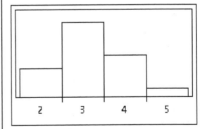

Equal treatment in the workplace	Count	%
2=Strongly disagree	7	19
3=Disagree	18	49
4=Agree	10	27
5=Strongly agree	2	5
Total	37	

The survey data is a starting point in terms of elucidating the story of resilience and success of African American women in science. A more detailed look at their stories is necessary to also explore their lived experiences. In Chapter 9, the findings from the survey are enriched through the shared stories of a selected number of African American women scientists who responded to the survey.

CHAPTER 9
Interview Findings

In this chapter, a subgroup of the survey respondents agreed to share their stories by participating in one-on-one interviews. Hatch (2007) described such stories as the second core theme of Critical Race Theory:

> The second core theme is that critical race theories are grounded in the lived experiences, unique experiential knowledge, and narrative voice of racialized and subordinated communities . . . . These lived experiences are not always reflected in the activities of scholars located in professional academia. . . . Not only have critical race theorists tended to emerge from subordinated social groups, their theories attempt to use the voices and experiences of people of color in the pursuit of social and economic justice. (p. 2)

The "voices" in this chapter are those of African American women scientists who believe that their experiences can help correct the imbalance of African American women in science. The case study findings are organized and presented using the following four variables, which are themes identified from the analysis of the interview data: parental involvement, academic experience, professional experience, and attributes for success in science. For purposes of anonymity, the voices behind the stories in this chapter have been changed to generic West African names.

Parental Involvement

Parental involvement, here, refers to the active engagement of parents and/or guardians in the education of the participants. Parental involvement has been shown to be strongly correlated with academic achievement (Epstein, 1995). Early involvement for African American parents relied on the relationships between African American parents and teachers. There was no formal organization *per se*; it was more a united front within the community. Starting in 1911, African American parents established and maintained their own organization, starting in Georgia, called Georgia Congress of Colored Parents and Teachers. The organization was so successful that in 1926, they held a convention to establish a national organization called the National Congress of Colored Parents and Teachers (Colley, 1999). As noted in Chapter 3, desegregation and the Civil Rights movement had negatives and positives. In this case, it was not until 1960, and an end to many of the Jim Crow laws, that the National Congress was able to meet and merge with its White counterpart to form one organization.

This integration with the White parent organization may have allowed for access to resources and increased membership, but what was lost was the concentrated focus and determination of African Americans to fight and struggle for equity in education. As urban schools grew and African American teachers in those schools decreased, administrators found ways to also limit the influence of parents. Luckily for many of the participants, African American parents were still very much engaged as they came through the school systems—both public and private. They may not have had as much influence on the schools or communication with teachers, but their involvement in the academic lives of their children tended to focus on the community and home.

In this study, participants were asked if their parents were involved in their education, and if so, to describe the level of involvement. All participants noted that their parents were involved in their education. Most of the participants describe how their mothers made sure that they did their school work, attended parent's nights, and provided support. In addition, they talked about their parents having high expectations of them regarding their performance in school and abilities to go to college.

The type of involvement is described by Sohna in the following passage:

> *I remember early on, when my mother was not working, she would make sure that we all sat down and did our homework when we came home. If there was, for example, any help that was required, she would just point us in the right direction. She would never find the answer and feed it to us. . . . If there was a subject we were doing poorly in, they expected that you would bring that grade up. Even when you did a good job, they weren't into giving presents or special things. It was just expected of you to do good in school. . . . So they gave their support in that way, but it was never to the point where they would take over and sit down and do homework for you. They just have never, ever done that.*
>
> *My father was kind of hands off. . . . I do remember one subject I had in high school, accounting, and he was an accountant. So you can imagine he took an interest in that. . . . He wasn't too involved in doing homework. He made sure we were enrolled in school and that school fees were paid. He was the one who took us to school every morning. . . . And again, he made sure we were enrolled in Catholic schools. He was very particular about where we went to school.*

Sohna's mother encouraged independence and inquiry by her children. There were no easy answers in life, so there would be none for homework either. This was one of the many ways parents armed their children with the skills they would need to navigate a system that would challenge them in more ways than they could imagine. Her father may not have been hands-on, but he was involved in making sure they had the best education he could pay for. Not only did they have to learn their letters, but they were also expected to come out at the top of their class.

Ramatoulie recalls the high level of expectation her parents had for her. Her mother was an English teacher at the high school in which she was enrolled, and her father was a professor in agriculture:

The only way I thought they were not so great is if you make an "A," why couldn't you make an "A+." That's the way they were. They just wouldn't be satisfied with just an "A" or something. You should do better. They expected more. Everything was expected. You were expected to finish high school with good grades. You were expected to go to college. You were expected to get some type of degree in something. Everything was expected. . . . My mother was a teacher at the high school where I went to school. She was very involved there. I remember them going to some PTA meetings, but I guess they would do more at home. Make sure we did our homework.

I know I'd have my mom look over my English papers and papers I had to write for my science class. Stuff like that. Then I'd ask my father to look over the content of the science part. My dad was good in math also, so he'd help us with our math.

The level of parents' education was not a factor in terms of encouragement and support. Parents understood that the school had to know that their children had advocates, and they were partners with the school in their children's education. Fatou's experience was similar to that of the other participants:

Neithr of my parents graduated from college, but were both very keen on education. I can remember quite vividly making it clear when we would go to parents' night at the beginning of the school year. . . . I can remember every year, without fail, they would make it a point to go to parent's night. Get to know our teachers, introduce themselves by name, make it quite clear that they were very supportive of what the teacher was doing. Basically, to just let the teacher know that if there were any problems, they were to contact them.

My parents were very big on education. One of the messages that I remember hearing again and again growing up is that you have to get a good education. Education is very important. You will get an education. This is important. School is not for fooling around or anything like that. Get a quality education. This is your ticket for future success. That was one of the clear messages.

As discussed in Chapter 3, the experiences and stories passed from generation to generation linked the fact that slavery denied access to education, Jim Crow laid down challenges to getting an education, and education was seen as a major path for parents to make sure their children did better than they did. Parents understood that the institutional racism in existence could only be overcome through education.

Many of the participants explained that it was their mothers who emphasized getting homework done. Fathers also gave encouragement, but their involvement was specific to certain tasks, such as "helping with math," "being supportive," and ensuring that "we were enrolled in school and that school fees were paid." There were exceptions, as Jainaba explains:

My parents were heavily involved in our education. Especially my dad. He's always pushed for the best grades possible, and made sure that he stayed on top of the school work we were doing in terms of looking at our homework, talking to our teachers to try and better our grades. He also would tutor us in math because he's an engineer. My mother helped out as well with a lot of tutoring, and the interactions with our teachers.

Parental involvement was also expressed as advocacy on behalf of the child at school. Three out of the seven participants gave specific examples of situations in which their parents intervened and advocated on their behalf at school. For example, of her mother's involvement, one of the participants noted:

She worked really closely with me. By second grade, I had pretty much had the homework routine down and didn't really need much help from that perspective. She pushed for us not to go to the neighborhood schools. We were actually bussed to schools in the White communities of New York, of Brooklyn. She attended most student activities, plays, whatever she could. She did work. She even pushed for me to play on the boys' basketball team when there was no girls' basketball team— although they didn't actually let me play, they just had me sit and watch from the sidelines. She pushed and said you have to create a fair opportunity for her.

Although the educational level of participants' parents ranged from no college education to graduate education, participants unanimously reported that their parents were fully involved in their education, thus suggesting that parental education level was not a factor in parental involvement in this specific sample. This determination that their children take full advantage of education, and the high expectations parents had were rooted in the strong desire that slaves and ex-slaves had for literacy. As Anderson (1988) recounted:

Blacks emerged from slavery with a strong belief in the desirability of learning to read and write. This belief was expressed in the pride with which they talked of other ex-slaves who learned to read or write in slavery and the esteem in which they held literate blacks. It was expressed in the intensity and the frequency of their anger at slavery for keeping them illiterate. "There is one sin that slavery committed against me," professed one ex-slave, "which I will never forgive. It robbed me of my education." (p. 5)

The fact that participants' parents uniformly emphasized the importance of getting an education is deeply rooted in African American history. During slavery, learning to read and write caused many to lose their lives. The constant reminders that their children had to do well, succeed, and meet high expectations in education, were founded on the strong belief and desire that slaves passed on from one generation to the next. Too much had been sacrificed in the struggle for the right to exercise the simple acts of reading and writing. Education was freedom.

Academic experience

Academic experience in this study refers to descriptions of participants' schooling (K–12), undergraduate, and graduate educational experiences. In terms of schooling, the experience that the participants share in common is that they were enrolled in some form of advanced or accelerated classes. In addition, field trips, after-school programs, summer science programs, and science-fair projects were threads that ran through the schooling experiences. For example, Sohna, who went through her K–12 education in a Caribbean country, recalled how field trips impacted her learning:

We started science education around 13 or 14. I distinctly remember my chemistry teachers. Biology, I remember that being very hands-on. There were a lot of demonstrations. I remember the teacher was very good at showing us what we were learning. Making it interesting. Chemistry, the same thing, very hands-on. Doing experiments. Even physics was very hands-on, too.

I don't remember the books being particularly good, but certainly, we had good teachers. We definitely took field trips when we could, especially the zoology class which was my first introduction to microbiology—which is my profession. We did field trips. I remember even going to the beach to look at marine life, looking at starfish and sea anemone and things like that.

For Kumba, the whole experience of getting into a specialty science high school she wanted did not work out for her as planned, and her junior high school counselors failed to tell her about a summer program. There was some disappointment, as she ended up in a school close to her home, but because of the accelerated classes, it really worked out to her advantage:

That was predominantly a very large, African American/Hispanic high school. Actually, all disappointment means is that something better comes around when one door closes. At Robeson High School I was in the accelerated class, and in advance courses and was exposed to a lot of programs for science and pre-med. I took the pre-med track, although I was the only one interested in veterinary medicine. They didn't have a veterinary medicine program, that's why I chose the pre-med.

Some of the participants had not planned on a life in the sciences, but were exposed to the subject because they were in the top 10% of their class, had tested into specialty schools, and/or were recruited because a summer program needed students of color. This was the case for Fatou:

At the time, the identity that I was forging was one of being one of the smart kids. I remember dealing with a lot of negative peer pressure. . . . I had the opportunity when I was in the eighth grade taking a placement test for a high school that was targeting kids who wanted to go on and prepare for technology careers. . . . That was a life saver. I really enjoyed my four years at the school . . . and it was a key factor in my schooling. It's interesting, in thinking back. I did well in science, but up until the 11th grade, I had thought I'd go into a career in law. . . . There was an internship program. . . . I think I was in the second year of the program. . . . So they went to the area high schools and they said, "We're going to have internships where the students will be working in the laboratory with the professor/mentor, and also doing a research project, research in the library. Do you know any students who might be interested? We'll put them up on campus for a week, in a dormitory so they get an idea of what college life is like. We'll have supervised activities for them. We'll also introduce them to these professors and technical people, and convince them to commit to a summer internship." I did that program and just loved it. It was great! It was my junior year in high school.

Haddy, like Fatou above, tested into a liberal arts school without a real focus on the sciences, but it was not until her junior year that a math teacher recognized her gift for math and suggested a summer school, at an Ivy League university, specifically for minorities. She did well, and pushed toward engineering. Access to the resources described above are key in terms of property rights—and intellectual property is part and parcel of that. Ladson-Billings and Tate explain (1995) how differences in those resources impacts education by telling the story of two young students who were preparing to enter high school. One of the students was going to a high school in an upper-middle-class neighborhood, while the other was entering a school in an urban, African American district. The differences in the curriculum choices were clear. For instance, the language choices in the upper-middle-class neighborhood included Spanish, French, German, Latin, Greek, Italian, Chinese and Japanese; while at the urban school only Spanish and French were offered. The gap in terms of numbers of choices was the same for math, science and electives. Ladson-Billings and Tate conclude:

> The availability of "rich" (or enriched) intellectual property delimits what is now called "opportunity to learn"—the presumption that along with providing educational "standards" that detail what students should know and be able to do, they must have the material resources that support their learning. Thus, intellectual property must be undergirded by "real" property, that is, science labs, computers and other state-of-the-art technologies, appropriately certified and prepared teachers. (p. 54)

As the Black women scientists in this interview reveal, they had access to those resources. Some as a result of the schools they went to, others because they had strong advocates who helped them identify the additional "property" they would need to succeed.

All of the women in this study expressed a love for learning in general, and a love for learning about science in particular. Jainaba found that her success in K–12 was linked to having a good anatomy teacher who made learning science easy and enjoyable:

> It has to be for my love for science. I enjoy it, which is something that definitely stands out for me. A lot of things I learned in school, I didn't care for. Such things like geography and history and some of the other subjects, but science was always something that I found very interesting and fascinating.

The smart track was not always easy. Ramatoulie describes being in the top of her class, but not popular. She was with the same students day in, day out; even their class schedules were different, so they did not mix with the students in the lower track. Her way out was in sports, but she always knew that her education track in K–12 would take her into higher education.

Because of the inequities within the system, or as Hatch (2007) pointed out, institutional racism, only a few African American children made it into the smart classes. Their African American friends, who were left out of the loop, ostracized them for being "smart." So their main source of encouragement was family.

Accelerated classes, field trips, after-school programs, enthusiastic teachers, and summer apprenticeships played a big role in the direction for these young Black women in science. Even with their preparation before the undergraduate education, it was not always an easy adjustment.

The nature of undergraduate experience varied by participant. Some participants were fortunate to have very supportive faculty, while others reported a feeling of isolation, as well as an obvious lack of support from academic advisors. For Sohna, that was demonstrated by her advisor's statement that she would not be able to complete such a rigorous program. Instead of backing away, Sohna dug deep and succeeded. She explains her experience when transferring from a smaller campus to the main campus of a state university system:

> When I went to sign up for the microbiology program, I met the head of the department and he was a Black man. He was also very encouraging, and that really helped me solidify my desire to study that subject more. But then, after the first year, he left to take an appointment elsewhere. When I transferred over . . . that's where I had the bad experience. The advisor who was assigned to me was a White Jewish female. . . . Basically, they tell you for the four years exactly what you should be studying. . . . So I show up for her just to sign my card. . . . And she said, "There's no way you can have all this workload!" And I was frankly very shocked . . . it was the first time she had ever met me! . . . I'm sure she took one look at me, and saw my Black face and decided I wasn't going to be able to do it. . . . But it had the opposite effect. . . . I think if I didn't have that inner strength and will power, it would have made me change my mind all together. I went on to do very well that semester and got "A's" and "B's."
>
> I was very happy at the end of the semester, to see her face. She was shocked! She said, "Well, I didn't think you could do this." I was sitting there smiling at her and thinking, "Yeah, right. I guess I showed you."

The above quote reminds us of the fact that one cannot assume that having a mentor and/or advisor of the same gender will guarantee that full support will be forthcoming. In this case, race overrode gender in the response of Sohna's advisor.

For those women who went to Historically Black Colleges and Universities (HBCUs), the challenge was in taking hard courses, not the environment. Kumba describes her experience at an HBCU as *"more of a nurturing environment. It was familial. It was a smaller school, and I had more African American teachers."* For Chumbey, even her undergraduate work at a mostly White university was made easier by supportive faculty. She was able to focus on her major and get advice and counseling regarding graduate school, but her experience was the exception, not the rule. Overall, with only a few minor bumps and challenges, the undergraduate experience was not exceptionally difficult.

Graduate education, however, presented other complications and challenges that were related to long hours, gender issues, difficult courses, lack of support inside programs, and having to find support outside of academia in family and friends. It was key to develop a sense of independence, self-reliance, discipline, and determination. Additionally, because of the need to study hard for long hours, some of the women felt isolated from their "own" because of their schedules and interests, and also shut out by their White colleagues socially, because it was one thing to work in the lab and classroom together, and another to party or hang out.

Ramatoulie's graduate experience began with a hangover from her undergraduate experience. Her K–12 education allowed her to develop strong relationships with White students, and she had not been exposed to the kind of racism the Black students she encountered in graduate school had experienced. She loved the outdoors and activities like hiking and skiing— which most of the White students were into, and the Black students at the time were actively engaging the racism on her campus. She felt that if she associated with the White students, her Black colleagues would abandon her, plus she found herself becoming more and more suspicious and angry. When asked what school was like at the graduate level, she explained:

> It was different but the same. I had become very, very hateful by my senior year. I decided that when I got to Vet school—again I was the only Black. They had one Black, one Hispanic, and one Asian per class. I decided I was basically going to be on my own. I was going to study and get through Vet school. My financial advisor even told me, he was honest enough to say, "You're going to do fine here academically, but it's going to be hard for you to make friends." Because he could see the racism, and he was White.
>
> I guess I got used to it. I just decided it wasn't going to bother me anymore. I got tired of hating. It's tiring, and it was affecting my health. So I decided, "Oh well, there's going to be jerks in the world, and there's nothing I can do about it."

This is where institutionalized racism can be seen. It is not necessarily written in the handbooks, but it is understood by the White majority that it is unnatural for African American women to follow a road to the sciences. Another thread that is woven through these stories is the feeling that they had to become self-reliant. Family would not always understand, even though they were supportive. Black friends might not be interested in the work you were doing, and White friends always let them know, after the fact, about parties or get-togethers. Yet, they would say, "No, we wanted you there." The question was always, So why was I not informed. Race was not always the issue in terms of "racism."

For Sohna, she purposefully chose a Black advisor, because during her first years as an undergraduate her Black advisor had been very supportive. She found a very different environment:

> *Actually, until I got to the PhD program, that was my first experience with having an advisor who was African American and not supportive at all. He was very—actually, it was a shock for me. I had no mentoring at all from this person. Yup, for the doctorate. Well, again, my own strong will and inner strength, I think, in that case. . . . It was kind of a slap in the face that he wasn't . . . well the issue with him was that I decided that I wasn't going into academia.*
>
> *I had not seen anything in academia that made me want to follow in anybody's footsteps. . . . I wanted to go into the food industry because, again, I wanted to be able to see the fruits of my labor. . . . My advisor, I think, was of the ilk that if you weren't going to go into academia and teach then you really weren't doing anything worthwhile. That was his perspective on things. . . . So, it was a slap in the face. I thought, well, I could get good mentoring from at least someone of the same race. But it didn't work that way. It was just, again, my fortitude and sticking with things and getting through.*

For Sohna, race was not an issue, but gender may have subtly played a role, in that her male advisor did not take her professional choice seriously. He was insensitive to her needs as a Black woman scientist.

A similar story is told by Fatou, who was enrolled in a master's level science program. She understood that the program would lead to a PhD, and that she would be working with the same White male advisor. As the program progressed, she realized that this was not going to work, as her advisor would have her redo projects, reverse his decisions, or change his mind about what she should do. She searched for and found a replacement advisor, but when she went to the graduate school to start the process, they told her she had to mediate the situation. At the meeting, her advisor told her, in an arrogant tone, that he already had a degree and that she was the one in need; further that he was the one in power and that her only choice was to do as she was told. The department took his side, explained that she had hurt his feelings, pressured the new advisor to drop out, and explained that without an advisor she would have to drop out of the program. When asked what role her gender and race played, she replied:

> *Well, I guess a part of my answer is that some might view it as speculative because I was the first woman of color graduate student in this department. From an historical perspective, there was no previous case to compare it to. That right there, I think, was something to be highlighted.*

Although she did not find an immediate solution when she went through the proper channels, she shared the issue with her independently formed support group—which in the end came to her aid. The matter was resolved and she moved on. Barres (2006) cited the need for women to be more vocal on their own behalf, and explained that the reasons they hesitate to speak out may lie in the lack of having secure positions (tenure). For graduate students, their position is even more untenable. There is no security. Even years after the fact, Fatou still frames her response as "speculative."

The theme of self-reliance is repeated by Jainaba, who went from an elite, mostly White school for her undergraduate studies to a HBCU. At the White school, she had to deal with a lot of overt racism; at the HBCU her experience was very different. When asked what her HBCU experience was like compared to the White institution, she explained:

> *Oh yes, very different! I was not prepared for that. . . . There wasn't the racism, of course, because everyone, for the most part, looked like me. Everyone was African American or a member of some other minority. Some of the issues I had, though, involved the fact that the PhD program there was in its infancy. A lot of things that should be in place in a program were not necessarily working at that point. . . . Other than that, it was a great experience for me. . . . If I hadn't gone to an African American School, I probably would have felt that this may not be the field for me, but I am definitely grateful for the fact that I had so many wonderful African American professors who pulled me aside and said, "Hey, don't give up. Just do it and get out there and be the best you can be. Just because you're an African American and also a woman does not mean that you are second-class to anybody."*
>
> *I felt as though my advisor cared a lot about me and some of the other graduate students. Unfortunately, I do not believe she knew exactly how to mentor students, which was very unfortunate. . . . She was away a lot dealing with family issues. . . . But it teaches you a lot. It teaches you to be more independent. It teaches you to think on your own, to troubleshoot on our own. Those are very, very valuable skills to have in this profession because you're not always going to have somebody to run to and consult with.*

For Jainaba, there is the intersection of gender and race. In the first instance, she describes her female advisor-mentor as caring, but not skilled as a mentor. Part of the issue is that her mentor is trying to balance her professional life with children and a family. Her husband travels a great deal, and family comes first. Instead of seeing this as an unfair gender issue, Jainaba exhibits her own gender biases by dismissing the family issues as less important than her mentor's professional responsibilities. Where race is intertwined in her experience is when she explains how her African American professors remind her to stay the course because she is not a second-class citizen. The idea that they would have to remind her of that goes back to Ladson-Billings and Tate's (1995) discussion of how inequality causes Blacks to feel deficient. They explained:

> As founder of the Association for the Study of Negro Life and History and editor of the Journal of Negro History, Woodson revolutionized the thinking about African Americans from that of pathology and inferiority to a multitextured analysis of the uniqueness of African Americans and their situation in the United States. His most notable publication, *The Miseducation of the Negro*, identified the school's role in structuring inequality and demotivating African American students.
>
> The same educational process which inspires and stimulates the oppressor with the thought that he is everything and has accomplished everything worthwhile,

depresses and crushes at the same time the spark of genius in the Negro by making him feel that his race does not amount to much and never will measure up to the standards of other peoples. (p. 50)

This deep-seated sense of inferiority is what prompted the faculty to remind Jainaba that she was not a second-class citizen.

Professional experience

The challenges do not end for these women once they have earned their advanced degrees, but they find that the struggles through the education system serve them well in the field. Haddy is very succinct in describing the ways her womanhood, Blackness, and science background merge and move her forward:

> Well, let's start with women. From the woman's perspective, I think those barriers are becoming less and less because there are more women proving they are capable. Now, there are still some dinosaurs out there. They still have the concept that women aren't able to do this. At my facility, I've seen that mindset change quite a bit. I actually like working with the guys.
>
> You know, playing sports have been one of the ways I've learned to compete with them, play with them, and be comfortable with them. So I'm comfortable working with largely a male team. We're joking right now because the current proposal I'm moving into is heavily dominated by women. . . . There've been a few jokes of people saying, "Hey, you guys got a lot of women going on that team." I heard estrogen versus testosterone.
>
> From a cultural perspective, as a minority—I think those barriers and stereotypes are starting to be dissolved. . . . I have never disinherited my background. . . . They see the way I dress. I occasionally wear the gray suit. Today, taking pictures, I had my little cool hat on that's going out for a magazine . . . and my braids. I don't disinherit that part of me. It also makes me capable of being a strong person, a strong Black female, as it so happens, but a strong person who stands up for what they believe. When I'm fighting with scientists over costs and what we can do and what we really can't do, I'm confident because I've gone through some trials and tribulations. . . . I've really come to realize that it is a strength, and I should not deny that. I need to embrace it at times and it can be helpful.

In this example, Haddy reflects on her position as a Black woman scientist, but explains that she has to "play with the boys" to help them understand, accept, and work with her. Barres (2006) told the story of early socialization of boys in terms of gender bias when the coach says something to the effect, "don't play like a girl." In this instance, Haddy temporarily, and unconsciously, hides her gender by using sports and playing like one of the guys. It is important to remember that the gender issues surrounding the perception of women's roles in science being unnatural because it was not feminine were in play across race. As a result, African American female scientists have to balance both gender and race in order to succeed.

For Jainaba, returning to the elite, White institution where acts of racism were something she experienced on a daily basis as an undergraduate is very different. Working from a position of power has allowed her to focus on her goals with a clearer understanding of how the status quo works, and how she can move beyond the barriers set in her path. As she explains,

> But being on this side, it's completely different. Having a degree and being in charge of your own thing is so much different than being an undergraduate just on your way. . . . I think I have a very good relationship with my mentor. As far as my other colleagues, I think I have a good relationship with them. I won't say very good because we just don't interact as much. Being the only African American female PhD there, I still feel a sense of doubt. I think that a lot of times it's not doubt because I don't know what I'm talking about. It's doubt because I'm an African American woman, and they're just not used to seeing a face that looks like mine in their setting.
>
> They're a little bit taken aback by it, but in general, they do a good job of trying to be politically correct and not get too out of hand. That's about it. The bottom line is it's still a White, male-dominated field. That's science, medicine, research—that's all of it. It's slowly but surely coming around. There are more PhD graduates coming out, more African American women coming out in this field. I think it will become a field in which African Americans, and in particular women, are comfortable or have made their mark.

One important thing to note is that, with all she has accomplished, she still cannot take ownership of the property she has earned—her position. She refers to her environment as "theirs," as she describes how "they" may not be used to seeing someone like her.

Not all of the women were able to follow their doctoral work into the laboratory or into the lecture hall. However, the training they received still served them in terms of the track they eventually took. Fatou explains, without regret, where the road took her:

> One of the things that was evident to me was that a lot of those academic positions were not out there; they were just not viable. I remember applying for a couple of academic positions before leaving school, thinking that I would have a good shot, and not even getting a first-round interview.
>
> So it became evident to me that trying to get a tenure-track position was not going to be easy. I had finished my thesis, turned everything in, and just decided to move back home, live with my folks, and take is easy for awhile as I looked for a position. That, right there, was a departure from what I think is the experience of a lot of students.
>
> Usually, by the time they file their dissertation, they have a postdoc or some sort of position lined up. Well, I didn't have that. . . . What I've done for the past six years has been more in the area of regulatory work, public policy type. All of the positions I've had have been non-laboratory positions. For all practical purposes, I have walked away from taking a laboratory, research, tenure-track type position. . . . I think the expectations of the time—the time of being in graduate school and doing a masters/PhD program—was: "Oh, when I finish, I'm going to go and be an assistant professor some place. Go to work in the industry as a scientist." Well, none of that happened. The positions I've held since leaving graduate school have been in a regulatory, public-policy type nature.

Many of the women explained their workplaces in terms of the specifics of what they do. The thread that runs through in terms of professional experience is that focus on the goals or job at hand remove the focus on being Black or a woman. Chumbey explained that because her company is very small and she is the only Black person with a PhD, everyone looks at her as if she is their equal. It is not that those pieces have faded into the background or are no longer relevant; it is the sense that these women have arrived, and they have very clear objectives to achieve for their various employers. Being able to afford travel, socializing, choosing your friends, where you want to live, who you want to associate with makes a difference when employed. As a student, there is a restriction in terms of what you must do to survive, and the people you rub shoulders with may not be those you choose, but those who are in the same position as you—White or Black, male or female.

Not all of the pieces fall into place, even with a double degree of DVM/PhD. Kumba started with a postdoc position and a supplemental grant. At the end of it, she decided to take a break because she felt burned out doing lab work. She was also interested in starting her family because she wanted a well-rounded life. She describes what her experience was pursuing a position at NIH:

> *I pursued NIH. However, with research at NIH, unfortunately, they have this network, I fall into the background of—I have the degrees. They're impressed with my degrees, but they said I needed more years of experience. The thing is with us, they want us to have all of this, but if you haven't been working for more than 10 years, you can't get something dealing with research administration and grant programs. It's like your dogged if you do, and dogged if you don't. With NIH, it's basically who you know. That's what I found at NIH. I pursued, I made great contacts.*
>
> *Basically, they would say, "Oh yeah, we'll look out for you." And all that stuff, but when it came to actually work on that, that didn't work. No, they didn't have anything. It was all empty promises. They smile, shake your hand, and then when it came time to offer you a position, they don't think about you. They already had someone else in mind. Yet, when people look at my resume, they're impressed with it. I've worked several places. Prestigious places, it wasn't like I didn't have great opportunities. But when it came time for actual jobs, hiring? Nothing. So it was kind of frustrating.*
>
> *The challenges gave me time to work on my spiritual life. I basically went toward a higher being. I'm very active in the church right now and that helps me stay grounded. This is not scientific, it may not sound scientific, but I basically put my hands in the Lord.*

Sohna's work experience was more positive. She started out in a laboratory setting, and was able to land a job in a corporation that allowed her to pursue a track in management or a track as a scientist. She chose the track for science.

> *Some days I actually have no idea what's going to come across my desk, who's going to be on the other end of the phone. In that sense, it's pretty exciting. It doesn't get boring. I haven't been bored at work. I think I can truthfully say I've never been bored just because of that. In terms of supporting R&D, that's one aspect of it.*

So the research projects are around real specific issues, real specific products in a lot of ways. There are some areas where it's real generic, but for corporate America your research projects are much more specific than in academia. You actually have a specific target in mind, and not just furthering the knowledge about something. It's really hard to say what you're going to be working on. For me, that's part of the excitement—it's not predictable at all.

The choice Kumba made worked for her and her love of science. She found a position that may have had its share of racist issues, but the work and her passion canceled out any negativity. In some cases it was a combination of negative experiences that led to positive outcomes. Ramatoulie described how, as a veterinarian in a really first-rate organization, she was unhappy.

I love the people I work with. That was very difficult in my first job. It was a first-class practice, but I didn't like the people. The receptionist was a racist. The doctors were racists. I realized that I couldn't work there, even though the money's better. I realized that you must like who you were with.

That's one thing I've found with this practice. It's not as fancy by any means. It's not as sophisticated. It's pretty poorly run. It could be run better. But I enjoy working with the people there, so that makes it very pleasurable.

Her ability to see the situation for what it was reflects what Johnson, Brown, Carlone, and Cuevas (2011) described regarding identity processes. Ramatoulie was able to change based on the identity she had forged for herself in the face of conflict. The challenges in education carry over into the workplace because the institutional racism is not the purview of one or two people, but an entire culture. It does not matter whether you are in academe, corporate institutions, or small practices, the issues are those that Critical Race Theory exhorts us to interrogate and change.

Attributes for success in science

If we understand some of the attributes these African American women scientists feel are important, then institutions of learning can put in place strategies that allow future female scientists to develop those attributes. When the question was put to the participants, they responded that patience, perseverance, and communication skills were key. As Chumbey put it:

Definitely have to be patient. A lot of times, projects or experiments are not going to work. You have to be determined, so that no matter what, you're going to keep on going and persevere through this. Good analytical skills are important. Attention to detail. You need to be able to write well and speak well—good communication skills.

Ramatoulie's advice related more to the early years of knowing you are smart and pursuing your interests in the face of peer pressure:

Make kids feel good about their studies. Talk to them about emotional things about how kids will keep them as an outcast because they're smart. Tell them it's okay. Make sure they don't feel bad about that.

A lot of kids will succumb to that. They'll act dumb on purpose. That's what I say with some of my friends. They would act dumb, and I would say, "You're smart. You don't have to fail the test to look a certain way." So you have to let them know that it's popular to be smart, and it's okay to be yourself. Stick to your guns and people will follow you. Don't give in to peer pressure.

Hard work. Stress that. It's hard work and it's okay to miss a party or two. Try and get jobs in your field to make sure you like it. Little things my mom told me, "Speak properly. Dress properly for the occasion." If you have a certain way you dress around your friends, that's fine. But you dress appropriately for that situation. So, those little things help so that you don't stick out as much. I'm not saying dress "White" or anything like that, I'm just saying dress properly for the occasion. Just be strong in what you like. Don't let people sway you or make you feel bad.

Ramatoulie's perspective speaks to many of the stories of what happens to young African Americans in high school when they are perceived by their friends as being too smart. Her bottom line is do not stick out, fade into the background. The opposite of that position was shared by Jainaba:

Strategies for success? Some of the same strategies I used as a graduate student. Surrounding myself with people who cared about me, people who want to see me do well. Reading a lot. That's pretty much the key. Being in the right place at the right time. Going to some of these meetings and conferences, even though you don't want to go. Getting your face out there and letting people know that you understand the matter at hand and you have input into whatever the discussion is. Basically, showing up and making your presence known, and making sure that you're never overlooked for someone who has the same credentials, the same background, and the same knowledge.

That takes a lot of just physical presence and being there and being accounted for. I think that, as women, as African American women in those settings, we have a tendency just to say, "Well, I don't belong." And not showing up. Just showing your face and letting them know that you are here.

Haddy emphasized inquiry and not being afraid to ask questions. For her, not being willing to inquire and ask did not bode well for success:

Inquiry is very important. The worse question is the unasked question. If you are not willing to inquire and ask questions, you can't be a good scientist. It's all about wanting to know why, understanding why. There's also the part about not being opinionated. It's true that you start out with a hypothesis, but you can't be so stuck to that hypothesis that what's staring you clearly in the face, the data or whatever you've collected to state your case, you're not willing to back off of what you initially assumed.

You have to be non-opinionated and look and see what you see in front of you. Being truthful. Teamwork. Hardworking. Inquisitive. I wouldn't say just qualities, I would say there are certain skills you need. You have to be a good communicator. Most people want to say, "Well, math and science. Math and science." No, you have to have good English skills (or other language). You have to have good verbal and written skills to communicate your ideas, your results, to sell your ideas, your results.

Fatou echoed the idea of having an inquiring mind. She relates that to research science and not accepting failure.

I think asking good questions, I would put at the top of my list. I guess also a sense of perseverance and tenacity. Research science can be very frustrating. The very development that makes you jump for joy one week, you can come back to the lab and try to replicate it and it just goes down the tubes. So I guess a sense of stick-to-itiveness. Being able to hang in there when the results are not as exciting as you would like all of the time.

Kumba highlighted being open and intelligent:

Very determined, competent, understanding, open-minded. That's very important, because people can be very closed-minded and can't see what's really going on. Studious, you have to be disciplined. It's not an easy route to go, so you have to be disciplined. And you have to be passionate—you have to love what you're doing. Of course, intelligence. We all have intelligence, you just have to know how to use your intelligence.

Being a female African American scientist is hard, just being African American anything is hard—well challenging, and we do what we can to overcome those challenges. People think that because of affirmative action you'll be able to get your foot in the door everywhere, but it really doesn't work that way. It's a challenge.

Sohna summed it up from the perspective of being a scientist, and echoed much of what her colleagues described:

Well, I think, just in terms of being a scientist—which is first and foremost what I consider myself to be—you need to have an inquisitive mind. Accepting the answer to a question isn't usually a quality of a scientist. A scientist wants to know more. And why. I think that's definitely a quality that's important. It's something natural. It's not something that you learn. It's just a natural quality. You want to understand more about a particular subject. You want to know why this is happening, and not just accepting the answer and maybe coming up with more than one answer other than the one that you heard or the one that you've read. So, first and foremost, an inquisitive mind.

Secondly, determination. You have to be determined to stick with something once you've started it. I think that's a quality everybody should have. You can't want to give up easily because—from a scientific perspective—answers don't come easily, they don't come quickly. It's a situation where you really have to have a sense of determination and stick-to-itiveness. Otherwise, you're not going to be successful.

Confidence is another quality. You've got to be able to rely on yourself; know who you are; know what you're capable of doing; know that you are capable of handling the tough things that come along and persevere.

So, perseverance is another one! I think, from the perspective of a female of African descent, for me it's always having to prove to myself that I am a scientist regardless of other labels. Of course, people look at you and say, "Well, she probably got there because of some quota. Or somebody felt sorry for her." Or something like that. So it's having to prove yourself—and it can be exhausting—but proving yourself everyday! Proving to yourself everyday that you're here because you know what you're doing.

All of the women involved emphasized the fact that being an African American woman was hard in itself, but being a scientist was even more challenging. They all acknowledged that it is not a perfect world, but their stories show a resilience that is a beacon to all comers. Most exhibited that spirit that refuses to fall, to give in, to turn away. The determination and fight that come from a history of struggle, regardless of what the institution or system may throw your way. So, in the end, who are these women? They believe that with gut-level determination you can succeed. Many of them are rooted in science and in religious faith. They do not see a conflict in believing in God and doing science. They were forged in families that helped them develop thick skins and the kind of skills that kept them putting one foot in front of the other in the face of adversity. These women were well aware of the institutional barriers set against them, but they did not give up, overall.

In terms of Critical Race Theory and the intersection of gender, race, and property or resources, it can be seen that gender and race continue to be key factors in the success rate for Black women scientists, and that woven throughout gender and race is access to and ownership of resources. However, it is important to further interrogate the system that continues to buffet African American women scientists and discourage them from continuing forward. Family, stories passed down through the generations, and a sense of determination have allowed these women to pursue and achieve their goals. In the final chapter, we review our findings and their policy implications.

CHAPTER 10

Framework for Success in Science and Policy Implications

In this book, we set out to investigate the academic and professional trajectories of African American women scientists. We were interested in answering the following questions: What are the personal characteristics and academic backgrounds of African American women scientists? What led them to careers in science? What academic trajectories did they follow? What professional trajectories did they follow? What factors contributed to their success in science?

Using a sample survey, case study, research synthesis, and the framework of Critical Race Theory, we found that African American women scientists are not a homogenous group, rather they are a diverse group in terms of age, marital status, academic and professional trajectories, factors attracting them to science, and factors contributing to their success in science. There were some commonalities, and the thread that runs through the case study is that their personal characteristics were overwhelmingly molded by family beliefs. All of the women interviewed told stories of how, by one means or another, they were raised to believe that education was a necessity. Not just any education, but choices that would put them in better stead than their parents. For some women scientists, the role models their parents projected were clear. They were the daughters of engineers, veterinarians, two generations of educators, and college professors. For some parents, the lack of a college education was the springboard that drove them to encourage, support, and push their daughters to do better. All of the parents wanted better lives for their children. Their parents were already keenly aware of the skills their daughters would need to navigate in a world that was set against them because of their race and their gender. The bar was raised high, in terms of the expectations their families had of them from early childhood into adulthood. Having been raised in this environment, the expectations they had of themselves were high as well. This is clear in the stories they tell of succeeding in spite of the low expectations of counselors and mentors. Even their African American classmates put pressure on them to participate in social activities and protests they had no time for; their isolation was compounded by their White classmates who did not allow them to participate in activities that would have supported their passion for science. Again, the character that was forged at the kitchen tables where they had to perform at the highest level armed them with skills to maintain that performance when family was elsewhere.

We also found that most of them went into science because they were exposed to the subject early during childhood, or were encouraged by either teachers or parents to develop inquiring minds. Two women, one from the Caribbean and the other from the southern US, describe teachers who cared deeply, who knew their families, who were better than any books in terms of engaging the minds of these young women. Others found their way into the sciences through honors programs, after-school programs, or summer workshops and camps. The exposure to thinking about how the world works; to trying to find solutions to where disease comes from, the origins of microbes, how things work—even in small ways—led them to the sciences. They were unafraid of science and math because their families never said, "you can't." African American women scientists talked specifically about the influences of science-enrichment experiences—such as involvement in after-school science programs, summer science programs, science-fair projects, and field trips—as major factors in getting them hooked on science.

Julie Haun-Frank (2011) used the exploration of everyday spaces to describe the trajectories of students who stay the course, in terms of lives in science. She discovered that school did not play as major a role as she had assumed. In addition to the spaces that influenced students' trajectories, she also looked at identity:

> Examining space as an aspect of identity work is valuable for bringing to the fore how sometimes nuanced factors such as social positioning, ideologies and other manifestations of power come to bear on individuals. Students construct understandings of who they are, who they want to become, and set goals about what they want to do in and with science. Social spaces such as school, home, and community mediate this identity work and in turn students enact a particular sense of who they are to organize and reorganize their trajectories. (p. 255)

In the previous chapter, it is very clear that the participants in this research study had developed strong identities that allowed them to do more than just reorganize their trajectories. They were willing to face their detractors and dare them to challenge the right to be in the mix. The families and communities the women in this study describe, and their determination to succeed, validate the idea of nuanced space as a major contributing factor to their success. The work of Johnson et al. (2011) also focused on identity. These researchers explained that because science is a high-status arena, there are benefits to its members not necessarily available in other fields. However, women coming from the "matrix of oppression" (p. 339) had to constantly negotiate their identities as women of color and science students, while having negative identities ascribed to them. They learned to read a situation quickly, make adjustments, and continue on their trajectory. This was also seen in the early history of women in science in general, and of African American women specifically.

For the women in this study, two types of factors were identified as contributing to their success in science at the undergraduate and graduate levels, namely contextual and environmental. As noted earlier in this book, the contextual factors were self-determination, family support, and religious faith, while the environmental factors referred to a healthy work environment with supportive supervisors and mentors. African American women scientists, through their stories, described the challenges of navigating the vast rainforest of science and sometimes having to rely on themselves. They talked about determination, self-reliance, and faith in God as their strategies for going through their education and training as scientists. Besides their stories of struggles and successes, African American women scientists experienced gender and race discrimination, but managed to rise above it.

From the findings, we learned about the academic and professional journeys of African American women scientists. All were exposed to explicit and implicit racism throughout their academic careers. One participant described how, by trying to balance her loyalty to her African American classmates and their struggle for equal treatment on their campus, she was becoming a hater of White people. In the lab and study groups, she was surrounded by those same White people, and realized that hating was not the issue. Her passion for science led her beyond that to a view of herself as a scientist and the road she had to take. Some respondents told stories of trying to learn in HBCUs where the facilities and programs were not quite up to par. However, having experienced the debilitating racism and low expectations in mostly White institutions, they chose to stay the course. HBCU faculty, fully aware that they were seen as an inferior choice, encouraged one respondent onward, and reminded her that she had the skills and knowledge to stand heads above everyone else.

Now, what framework for success can we recommend? What are the likely implications for policy and practice for such a framework? In the rest of this chapter, we will outline a framework for success in science, along with its underlying assumptions, limitations, and policy implications.

Framework for success in science

Based on what we have learned from our study and from those that came before us, we believe that a framework for success in science should focus on the following components: early exposure during childhood to hands-on science activities; parental involvement in science education in particular and education in general; access to and ownership of science resources; supportive academic advisors and mentors; and a workplace that is free from gender discrimination and institutional racism. All of these have economic implications for educational systems.

Early exposure

We recommend that in their formative years, children should be engaged in hands-on science activities that expose them to the content and process of sciences. This requires that Head Start teachers, nursery school teachers, and early childhood teachers have training that allows them to facilitate learning beyond reading, writing, and gaining social skills. Certification programs for those who run early childhood centers should include how to use nature walks to help young children develop inquiring minds by turning over logs, lifting stones, and in urban areas, paying attention to what lives in the cracks of the sidewalks and in holes in the playground. There are insects everywhere, and they outnumber us in both urban and rural areas. Capturing even one and examining where it lies in the food chain, or investigating the positives or negatives of that one insect, can change the awareness of a child when it bats away that mosquito or looks at the fly or roach on the wall. If early childhood educators are not skilled in place-based education and hands-on, project-based education, they will smother a child's natural curiosity with heart shapes and pumpkin shapes and snowflake shapes to cut and color. Their training has to include HOW to conduct a field trip to the museum so that children learn through all of their senses about what they are seeing. Children's museums are tremendous places to have that experience, but if an early childhood educator is not comfortable him or herself in that environment through lack of exposure, then field trips cannot capitalize on the excitement the children feel at going someplace new. Leaves and seashells are free and available for collecting.

Before a state certifies or licenses someone as an early childhood educator, therefore, clear requirements, in terms of expectations, need to be set by certifying agencies. It is not enough to have a bachelor's degree in early childhood development. That also has implications for colleges and universities. Programs that are accredited by outside agencies need to be able to show evidence that their curricula go beyond the basics. Local agencies or state agencies have to develop and implement workshops and certification programs for those early childhood specialists who are already out in the field. Again, all of these recommendations require money, but for many children, these first incursions into school are key in their development, especially if they come from homes where the encouragement and support are not there. This list is partial. The thing to remember is that it is important to find low-cost and economic ways to expose children to science. These suggested activities can be done in urban, suburban, and rural settings, as well as in or outside of school. However, the facilitators have to be trained in order to implement these activities.

At the elementary through upper grade levels, students can be exposed to science through guest speakers, science fairs, access to science equipment and/or laboratories, technology-based projects, and after-school science programs. This implies that the institution has a budget that will allow for this and space for properly equipped laboratories or work areas. For elementary school teachers, because they have to teach everything, collaboration with outside organizations is necessary. Partnerships can be formed with local, science-based institutions or universities to create science-enrichment programs for students. Hahn-Frank (2011) described the students in her study as part of a school within a school. Acceptance into the program was competitive, so there was already an early desire of these students to succeed. But schools within schools also require budgets to run and sustain them. We are assuming that there will be funding to support such partnerships, and that there will be qualified and motivated science teachers who will create the curricula to support these programs. At the same time, there should be administrators and/or principals who are supportive and aware of the importance of early exposure. The principals and teachers must also have a relationship of trust that will allow teachers to take risks and try new ways of teaching science. It cannot be "by the book" learning. The cultural institutions involved also have to have monies budgeted for staff to maintain the partnerships, and should also host professional development workshops for learning how to create projects for K–12 students. Whole communities have to come together—businesses, museums, schools, administrators, and families.

Parental involvement

As indicated in this study, parental involvement is key to the success of African American women scientists. It is important to add that involvement can take many forms. For instance, it could be a legal guardian, grandparent, aunt, uncle, or adopted parent who is responsible for raising the child. What is key is that this parent and/or family member is convinced of the importance of education in general, and supportive of the child's choice of science education in particular. It is extra helpful if the parent or guardian has a knowledge or some training in the sciences or education, but it is not necessary. What is required is an understanding that their support has a major effect on their child's level of success. The stories the participants shared about their parents' involvement highlight the key role parents play. Many of the families were advocates for their children, in terms of making sure that they had a fair opportunity. They were also implicit advocates by showing up to family night; introducing themselves to the teachers and administrators; and making sure the schools understood that they were partners, but also concerned about their daughters' education.

For a school or community, this may mean providing services for parents who do not have the resources or maybe the knowledge base to offer particular kinds of support. The integrated school movement proposes that schools be open after hours, and that they develop relationships with lawyers, doctors, social workers, and community activists. This trend is helpful to parents, who may sometimes feel that the school is more of an enemy than an advocate. The implications again mean financial inputs from already stretched school districts. Many schools offer opportunities to parents to become teacher-aides and to assist in the classroom. However, for parents who work two jobs, or have younger children they have to care for because they cannot afford child-care costs, this option is not feasible. Outreach programs, again from the schools to the families, are needed, and this is where the integrated school model could work.

Enrichment programs should include workshops for parents, where they meet to discuss and learn how to help their child succeed in science. There should also be presentations given by their children, so the parents can actually see the advantages of encouraging and supporting their child in this learning process. Because our focus is on gender and women in science, it cannot be emphasized enough that parents want their female children to believe they can achieve anything. Schools or enrichment programs may also have to develop brochures and newsletters, or hold workshops on gender and race issues for young women who want to pursue a career in science. This assumes that these activities will be scheduled at a time when parents can actually participate.

There is also the issue of resettlement centers for families fleeing political oppression and wars. Language and cultural barriers have to be hurdled. Community centers that operate after hours are also resources that can be used to help families with language issues, culture shock, and economic and housing challenges. Coming sometimes from societies where inquiry and speaking out are not part and parcel of cultural development, the idea of advocating for themselves or their children is not a consideration. This is one of the areas where the issue becomes complex. Being able to understand the culture—to read, write, speak, and think in the language of the culture—has to come first for these parents. Their children, far more adaptable than they are, will speed ahead. Finding ways to allow children to become their parents' teachers is another way to broadcast the belief that we need all women of color to consider science fields as a professional choice.

Parents are their children's first teachers, and there have been major improvements in the ways schools have partnered with parents to improve the academic learning of their children. However, it will take time for many schools that for decades have held a deficit model of parents and their ability to be involved (Colley, 1999). For many parents, especially in urban schools, their first entrance to the building is through a security guard who sits at the gate. The second encounter is through a window or over a counter with the school's administrative staff. They are usually called to the school when something is wrong, or when their child needs testing, or fees are missing. This negative first encounter creates an attitude within parents that is counterproductive. They want their child to do right so that they do not ever have to come to the school for any reason except to pick up their child and bring them home. Parental involvement in schools is still a work in progress, and again, it means time and economic inputs to change the status quo.

Science resources

What do we mean by science resources? This term is used here to include both tangible and intangible resources. By tangible, we mean access to well-equipped and up-to-date laboratories, libraries, museums, scientific tools and materials, technology, transportation, and chaperones. Intangible resources include tutors, mentors, school counselors, and a supportive and safe community.

These resources are critical for inspiring students to pursue science. However, all of these resources come at a cost. Without them, there is no opportunity for students to have a real-world, science experience. Our assumptions here are that the community—be it a school, enrichment program, or community center—has the economic resources to provide access; that businesses are willing to offer and/or donate goods, services, volunteers, or money to support the teaching and learning of science; and that some kind of local or state funding will be available to subsidize these activities.

However, it is important to point out that one of the intangible resources is the ability of a teacher to look out his or her window and understand that he or she can teach science using place-based resources. What is just outside the door? Is there grassland, woods, a park, the sidewalk, and a weed-filled playground? If the teacher avails his or herself of the information and resources that are free, then the issue of added dollars becomes moot. It then becomes an issue of curriculum requirements and administrators who are willing to allow teachers to do what most of them are trained to do—use creativity to advance learning. This strategy turns a whole community into a learning center for the students in this classroom. It does not cost anything to take a walk around the block and do a survey of all of the activities that can be used to teach science. Teacher-training programs and professional-development workshops can enhance this kind of hands-on learning. As Sohna reminded us, it was rock and shell collections and field trips into her community that started her down the road to being excited by learning about science.

Advisors and mentors

In order to succeed in science at the college level, it is critically important that students have access to advisors and mentors who will guide them through their academic careers successfully. Advisors must be knowledgeable, be advocates for their students, and be able to channel them to the appropriate programs, and most importantly, provide them with both academic and moral support. Mentors, on the other hand, are critical in the training and facilitating of the acquisition of science-process skills. The assumption for mentors is that they are willing and able to guide students from the beginning to the end of their program or project. We also assume that there are guidelines in place for the selection of mentors, placement of students, and clear articulation of roles and responsibilities. In order for mentoring to be successful, colleges and universities should make every effort to match mentors and mentees based on mutual interests and goals. Issues of race, ethnicity, gender, sexual orientation, religion, and nationality should be openly negotiated to ensure compatibility.

However, these issues cannot be negotiated if the institutions have not put in place opportunities for faculty to honestly and safely interrogate the history of how those issues have come into play in academia. Hatch (2007) described Critical Race Theory as "a historical and contemporary body of scholarship that aims to interrogate the discourses, ideologies, and social structures that produce and maintain conditions of racial injustice" (p. 1). This is a long-term process, because it also requires the investigation of White privilege. If an institution cannot provide a safe place for these conversations, then the road to success for African American women scientists will remain a major challenge.

Gender discrimination and institutional racism

Discrimination and racism have always existed in one form or another, but beginning around the 1800s, they were given credibility by scientists and scholars who used their expert status to promote unscientific theories about the nature of women and the inferiority of non-White cultures. Lipsitz Bem (1993) described gender discrimination as follows:

> Throughout the history of Western Culture, three beliefs about men and women have prevailed: That they have fundamentally different psychological and sexual natures, that men are inherently the dominant or superior sex, and that both male-female differences and male dominance are natural. (p. 1)

This indictment is critical in understanding how, in Western culture, women have been so objectified and marginalized when it comes to active participation in science particularly, and societal progress in general. The attitudes toward racism are equally damning, as can be seen in the following pronouncement by Louis Agassiz (1807–1873), a prominent scientist and intellectual of his time at Harvard:

> Although legal equality must be granted to all, blacks should be denied social equality lest the white race be compromised and diluted: social equality I deem at all time impracticable. It is a natural impossibility flowing from the very character of the negro race (10 August 1863); for blacks are indolent, playful, sensuous, imitative, devoted, affectionate in everything unlike other races, they may but be comparable to children, grown in the stature of adults while retaining a childlike mind. . . . Therefore, I hold that they are incapable of living on a footing of social equality with the whites in one and the same community, without being an element of social disorder (August 1863). Blacks must be regulated and limited, lest an injudicious award of social privilege sow later discord. (as cited in Gould, 1996, p. 80)

Although the 1800s did not usher in these ideas, as they existed long before, they became imbedded in the consciousness of the dominant culture of a new nation. Even though a lot has changed since then, we are still battling these attitudes today in different shapes and forms. The stories of the African American women in this book offer evidence that there is much to be done in terms of fighting against gender discrimination and institutional racism in the workplace. Ladson-Billings and Tate (1995) noted that understanding the intersection of race and property or resources allows us to see more clearly the action we must take, and we contend that for African

American women in science, it is the intersection of gender, race, and property that will lead us on a path to understanding how to increase the success rate of these women in the sciences. It is no easy task, as Bell (2004) elaborated:

> Today, black people and many Hispanics are trapped in a racial time warp. We are buffeted by the painful blows of continuing bias as the law upon which we relied for remedies is reinterpreted by unsupported assurances that the disadvantages we suffer must be caused by our deficiencies because, we are told without even a trace of irony, racism is a thing of the past. The hypocrisy so apparent in the claims of a color-blind society illustrates the harsh and disconcerting truth about racial progress. We prefer to ignore or rationalize rather than confront these truths because they disrupt our long-settled expectations of eventual racial equality. (p. 187)

The same can be said for gender inequities. The founding fathers wrote the law in such a way that Blacks, women, and children were objects, with no apparent rights, who could be moved, disposed of, and ignored without consequence. Today, one of the few ways in which the status of Black women in science will change or improve is for each to raise the alarm when sexism and racism raise their heads in the workplace. This is no easy task, and will require support from the leadership of the institutions in which Black women scientists work. It will also require these Black women scientists to organize and present a united front to fight and change the policies that allow these kinds of inequities. They must "lift every voice" and let their voices be heard across all levels of society.

America must also take full responsibility and renew its commitment to eradicating discrimination and institutional racism. During the past half a century, we have seen landmark US Supreme Court decisions such as Brown v. Board of Education of Topeka, Kansas, and the passing of laws (Civil Rights Act of 1964 and Voting Rights Act of 1965), designed to right the wrongs of the past. We have seen even the election of a two-term Black President, and there are some people who believe that we are now living in a post-racial America. Although the vision of a post-racial America may be true for some Americans and a good thing for the country, the reality today for most African Americans is that even though we have achieved progress in fighting racial inequality and injustice, some things have remain unchanged. Race still acts as a determining factor in educational and economic attainments. Most national social, economic and political indicators point to this reality. High profile Supreme Court rulings and Congressional legislations alone are not enough. There must be consistent, long-term investments and commitment to solving the problem. As Robinson (2000) puts it:

American capitalism, which starts each child where its parents left off is not a fair system. This is particularly the case for African Americans, whose general economic starting points have been rearmost in our society because of slavery and its long racialist aftermath. American slaves for two and a half centuries saw taken from them not just their freedom but the inestimable economic value of their labor as well, which, were it a line item in today's gross national product report, would undoubtedly run into the billions of dollars. Whether the monetary obligation is legally enforceable or not, a large debt is owed by America to the descendants of American slaves.

Here too, habit has become our enemy, for America has made an art form by now of grinding its past deeds, no matter how despicable, into mere ephemera. African Americans, unfortunately, have accommodated this habit of American amnesia all too well. It would behoove African Americans to remember that history forgets, first, those who forget themselves. (p. 231)

All indications are that we still have a lot of work to do in terms of encouraging resilience and success in this field. The stories in this book offer a source of inspiration that must be supported and encouraged in those building on this foundation.

Compensation and reward system

When it comes to the issue of race and gender in STEM fields, our compensation and reward system is broken, and needs to be fixed. As alluded to earlier in Chapter 4, the Lilly Ledbetter Fair Pay Act passed by President Obama in 2009 is a step in the right direction. However, a lot more work on equal pay for equal work remains to be done. Business, industry, and institutions of higher education, where most African American women scientists and engineers received their training and also are employed, must take the lead and set examples. Salary and compensation scales should be made available at the time of hire and there should be transparency on what academic background and qualifications are worth in terms of base salary and what added value compensation is worth in terms of professional experience. So for instance if two candidates are hired at the same time with very similar academic background and skill sets, they should be compensated the same at the time of hiring. Any differences in compensation should be disclosed and reasons provided. Human Resource Departments should be empowered to provide all hired candidates with the information required to demand a fair salary and to take action when a hired candidate feels unfairly treated. This will enhance and strengthen already existing regulations and the work of EEOC personnel. Those in leadership positions such as presidents, provosts, deans, chief scientific officers, CEOs, senior scientists/engineers, principal investigators, senior tenured professors, department heads, and trustees all have a role to play in ensuring that junior women scientists and mid-career women scientists receive fair pay.

A closely related issue to fair pay for African American women scientists and engineers, particularly in academic science, is tenure. Tenure in academia could be traced back to the late 1800s when "...nearly 10,000 teachers from across the country met in Chicago for the first-ever conference of the National Educator's Association....The topic of 'teacher's tenure' led the agenda. By the turn of the century, tenure had become a hot-button issue that some politicians preferred to avoid" (Stephey, 2008, p. 2). In 1915, the American Association of University Professors (AAUP) published its Declaration of Principles on Academic Freedom and Tenure report (AAUP, 2013a). In it the authors stated "Academic freedom in this sense comprises three elements: freedom of inquiry and research; freedom of teaching within the university or college; and freedom of extramural utterance and action" (p. 292). However, there were no specific guidelines on the subject of tenure until 1940 when the association published its 1940 Statement of Principles on Academic Freedom and Tenure (AAUP, 2013b). This document for the first time outlined a road map that institutions of higher education should follow for the tenure process. It specifically identified a probationary period (seven years) on a tenure track, freedom of teaching and research and a tenure period that guaranteed economic security.

Today most research universities and four-year colleges have some form of tenure process. For African American women scientists and engineers, the tenure process is not always straightforward and remains elusive. An unnamed senior tenured faculty of color once told one of the authors of this book that tenure is 60 percent effort and 40 percent politics, but for most of us is one 100 percent effort and one 100 percent politics, which is unattainable. Hence you don't see many of us in academia as tenured faculty. We have seen in Chapter 4 that when we looked at the data on who gets tenure by science and engineering field, we found that across the board, African American women scientists are grossly underrepresented in the ranks of tenured faculty. More needs to be done by making the tenure process transparent, less political and a competency-based process. Tenure committees must be representative of the community of faculty and students they serve, and accountable for their decisions. An appeals process must be taken seriously and fully supported at all levels. Tenure should be earned and not given away based on influence and favoritism. What is important to realize is that in academic science, those who get tenure have more economic security, academic freedom and access to resources, all of which are essential ingredients for success in science. African American women scientists and engineers must be supported from the moment they enter a science career all the way to earning tenure. For only in this way can we increase the numbers of tenured scientists and demonstrate to those young women scientists who want to follow the footsteps of their role models, mentors, teachers, and parents that it is worth pursuing science in academia.

Concrete solutions

Looking at the whole picture as described above creates a complex matrix of interlocked traditions, beliefs, and practices. It seems overwhelming, in terms of resolving the problem of the paucity of African American women in science. There is hope. Academia needs to interrogate the curricula used to train science teachers. Are they being trained to meet the standards for each state? Are they focused on the most recent edict of the Common Core that will be nationally based? Is there any aspect of the curricula that takes a concentrated look at how science teachers can be trained to support and encourage their future students—specifically their African American female students—to pursue careers in science. Changes in the focus of curricula at that level can create a sea change in increasing the numbers of African American women moving into the field. That is achievable, as long as there is the will.

It is not just science classes in school that expose future scientists to the field. There are few communities that do have some community center or after-school or summer programs that are located nearby. Scientists already in the field must reach out and help establish programs that expose young girls to the excitement of developing inquiring minds. In urban and rural areas, Boys & Girls Clubs, the Girl Scouts of America, YWCAs, libraries, civic centers, local farms and farmers, and community organizations can provide a space for the development of local programs that can implement hands-on, project-based, place-based programs at little or no cost. Role models are key, and the payback is one on which no monetary value can placed.

Science and social studies have been marginalized by a focus on literacy and math. But there is social studies in science, art, literacy, and a ton of math. If institutions of education train teachers to think across disciplines, then science can be integrated into the lessons of the day across disciplines, not just once a week or when there is a field trip. Science takes place all around us every moment that we breathe.

There is hesitation in connecting science with domestic duties, for fear that it will harken back to the days when women were only considered in terms of what they did in the home. The downside of that attitude is that children are exposed to science in the home implicitly, but it could be more explicit, by looking at the science of cooking; how an ingredient goes from a liquid state to that of a solid or gas; what are the physics of refrigeration; what are the characteristics of yeast cells, and how do they make bread rise; what does the food in packages at the grocery story look like when it is planted in the ground or walking around on four legs. Where does the soil in which plants grow come from? Why is pH something to consider at home and elsewhere? The possibilities are endless, and parents can play a role if teachers make questions like this part and parcel of the homework students are assigned.

Science teaching and learning in schools and afterschool programs should mirror the way science is practiced in the real world. This means that teachers and facilitators of science must be provided with pre-service training and/or professional development in inquiry-based teaching strategies such a project-based science (Colley, 2008). Project-based science instruction allows students to investigate their surroundings and communities by posing questions that are relevant to their own lives, and conducting real-life projects. During project-based learning, students collaborate with each other and with local scientists, use computers and scientific tools, collect and analyze data, prepare and present reports for peer review. Teachers and facilitators serve as leaders, mentors and advisers during the learning process. Students learn science by "doing" science. As our participants have indicated in Chapter 9, most of them were exposed to science and eventually hooked by the "doing" part.

We have seen how devastating the racist and gender biases can be when women and African American women are left out of the mix. Worse yet, it is a tragedy, when we consider how many contributions have been made and have gone unacknowledged. The women who participated in this study have succeeded in their efforts, and they stand as proof that the possibilities are greater than what is declared "impossible." A change in attitudes, the tearing down of the walls of misinformed stereotypes, and a constant consciousness and awareness of gender bias and racism in our institutions can remove many of the barriers present. But there are resilient and determined African American women who will continue to forge pathways to science. We just need to widen those pathways so that it is not a trickle, but a flood.

APPENDIX I

Race, Gender, and Science Survey

1. Personal History

a. Age group

		b. Marital status	
0–35	☐	Married	☐
35–45	☐	Unmarried	☐
45–55	☐	Single	☐
55–65	☐		
65–75	☐		
More than 75	☐		

2. Academic Background

a. What type of school did you go to?

		b. Degrees earned	
Public	☐	BS	☐
Private	☐	MS	☐
Parochial	☐	PhD	☐
Others: _____		Others	☐
		Please indicate: _____	

c. What type of after-school and/or extracurricular activities did you engage in when you were in school?

Baseball/softball	☐	Yearbook	☐	Summer job	☐
Basketball	☐	FFA/FTA, etc.	☐	Debate club	☐
Soccer	☐	Student council	☐	Community service	☐
Swimming	☐	Hobby societies	☐	University-sponsored programs	☐
Cheerleading	☐	Museum	☐		
Music	☐	Mentoring	☐	Exchange programs	☐
Drama club	☐	Tutoring	☐	Foreign travel	☐
Science fairs	☐	Public library	☐	Others: _____	
Honor society	☐	Field trips	☐		
Newspaper	☐	Internship	☐		

d. Who contributed most toward your education?

Father	☐	Uncles/Aunts	☐	Others	
Mother	☐	Brothers/Sisters	☐	Please indicate: _____	
Both Parents	☐	Teachers	☐		
Grandparents	☐	Friends	☐		

e. Who contributed most toward your science education?

Father	☐	Uncles/Aunts	☐	Others	☐
Mother	☐	Brothers/Sisters	☐	Please	
Both Parents	☐	Teachers	☐	indicate: [____]	
Grandparents	☐	Friends	☐		

f. Discipline

Agriculture	☐	Material Science	☐
Biology	☐	Medical Science	☐
Chemistry	☐	Microbiology	☐
Climate Science	☐	Neuroscience	☐
Earth & Environmental Sciences	☐	Paleontology	☐
Engineering	☐	Physics	☐
Food/Nutritional Sciences	☐	Planetary Science	☐
Forestry	☐	Plant Science	☐
Geochemistry	☐	Space Science	☐
Health Science	☐	Wildlife Conservation	☐
Immunology	☐	Others: [____]	
Marine Science	☐		

3. **Professional Trajectories**

a. Career path

Government	☐
Industry	☐
University/College	☐
Not-for-profit	☐
Private	☐
Others	☐
Please indicate: [____]	

b. Experience

Less than 5 years	☐
10–15	☐
15–20	☐
20–25	☐
25–30	☐
More than 30 years	☐

c. Primary responsibility

Administration/ management	☐
Research & development	☐
Teaching	☐
Postdoctoral	☐
Marketing/Service	☐
Others	
Please indicate: [____]	

d. What made you choose to become a scientist or pursue a career in science?

_____

e. What factors contributed to your success in graduate school?

_____

f. What factors contributed to your success as a scientist in the workplace?

_____

g. What were the main challenges you faced in pursuing a career in science?

_____

h. How did you overcome your challenges?

_____

i. What do you consider to be the most important qualities of a scientist?

_____

Please rate your level of agreement with the following statements:

4. As an African American woman scientist, I have experienced race and gender discrimination in the workplace.

1. No opinion	2. Strongly disagree	3. Disagree	4. Agree	5. Strongly agree

5. As an African American woman scientist, I am treated equally to my other colleagues in the workplace.

1. No opinion	2. Strongly disagree	3. Disagree	4. Agree	5. Strongly agree

APPENDIX II

African American Women Scientists Study Interview Guide

1. Could you describe your family background for me?

2. In what ways were your parents involved in your education?

3. Can you describe your elementary, middle, and high schooling?

4. When did you first get interested in science and what motivated you to pursue science?

5. Can you describe your college education?

6. What were your strategies for success, and challenges in pursuing science at the undergraduate level?

7. What were your strategies for success, and challenges in pursuing science at the graduate level?

8. Can you describe the positions you have held as a scientist, including your current one?

9. What are your strategies for success as a career female African American scientist?

10. What are your challenges as a career female African American scientist?

11. If science educators want to help students become successful in science or become scientists, what qualities should we try to instill?

12. Do you have any comments you want to add that will help in the understanding of African American females in science?

Sources

Adamson, L. B., Foster, M. A., Roark, M. L., & Reed, D. B. (1998). Doing a science project: Gender differences during childhood. *Journal of Research in Science Teaching, 35*(8), 845–857.

Adenika-Marrow, T. J. (1996). A lifeline to science careers for African American females. *Educational Leadership, 53*(8), 80–83.

Adigwe, J. C. (1992). Gender differences in chemical problem solving amongst Nigerian students. *Research in Science and Technology Education, 10*(2), 187–201.

Allen, E. J. (2003). Constructing women's status: Policy discourses of the university women's commission reports. *Harvard Education Review, 73*(1), 44–72.

American Association of University Women. (2010). Why so few women in science, technology, engineering and mathematics. Washington, DC: Author.

American Association of University Professors. (2013). APPENDIX I: 1915 Declaration of principles on academic freedom and academic tenure. Retrieved on April 11, 2013 from http://www.aaup.org/report/1915-declaration-principles-academic-freedom-and-academic-tenure

American Association of University Professors. (2013). 1940 Statement of principles on academic freedom and tenure with 1970 interpretive comments. Retrieved on April 11, 2013 from http://www.aaup.org/file/principles-academic-freedom-tenure.pdf

American Federation of Teachers. (2011). Promoting racial and ethnic diversity in the faculty: What higher education unions can do. Washington, DC: Author

Anderson, J. D. (1988). *The education of Blacks in the South, 1860–1935*. Chapel Hill, NC: University of North Carolina Press.

Antioch College. (2012). Mission and history. Retrieved from http://antiochcollege.org/about/mission_and_history.html

Armstrong, K. (1994). *A history of God: The 4000-year quest of Judaism, Christianity, and Islam*. New York, NY: Ballentine Books.

Armstrong, K. (2007). *Muhammad: A prophet for our time*. New York, NY: HarperCollins.

Atwater, M. M. (2000). Females in science education: White is the norm and class, language, lifestyle, and religion are nonissues. *Journal of Research in Science Teaching, 37*(4), 386-387.

Baker, D. (1986). Sex differences in classroom interactions in secondary science. *Journal of Classroom Interaction, 22*, 212–218.

Barres, B. A. (2006). Does gender matter? *Nature, 442*(7099), 133–136. doi:10.1038/442133a

Beaton, A. E., Martin, M. O., Mullis, I. V. S., Gonzalez, E. J., Smith, T. A., & Kelly, D. L. (1996). Science achievement in the middle years: IEA's third international mathematics and science study. Chestnut Hill, MA: TIMSS International Study Center, Boston College.

Becker, B. J. (1989). Gender and science achievement: A reanalysis of studies from two meta-analyses. *Journal of Research in Science Teaching, 26*(2), 141–169.

Bell, D. A. (1992). *Faces at the bottom of the well: The permanence of racism*. New York, NY: Basic Books.

Bell, D. A. (1995). David C. Baum Memorial Lecture: Who's afraid of Critical Race Theory? *Illinois Law Review*, (4), 895-908.

Bell, D. A. (2004). *Silent covenants: Brown v. Board of Education and the unfulfilled hopes for racial reform*. New York, NY: Oxford University Press.

Belotti, E. G. (1975). *Little girls*. London, UK: Writers and Readers Publishing Cooperative.

Berea College. (2012). The Berea story. Retrieved from http://www.berea.edu/about/history/

Bergland, R. L. (2008). Urania's inversion: Emily Dickinson, Herman Melville, and the strange history of women scientists in nineteenth-century America. *Signs, 34*(1), 75–99.

Bhattacharyya, S., Nathaniel, R., & Mead, T. P. (2011). The influence of science summer camp on African American high school students' career choices. *School Science and Mathematics, 111*(7), 345–353.

Bleier, R. (1988). The cultural price of social exclusion: Gender and science. *NWSA Journal, 1*(1), 7–19.

Bolden, T. (2004). *The book of African American women.* Avon, MA; Adams Media.

Bransky, J., & Qualter, A. (1993). Applying physics concepts—Uncovering the gender differences in assessment of performance unit results. *Research in Science and Technology Education, 11*(2), 141–155.

Brophy, J. E., & Good, T. L. (1974). *Teacher-student relationships: Causes and consequences.* New York, NY: Holt, Rinehart and Winston.

Buffery, A. W. H., & Gray, J. A. (1972). Sex differences in the development of spatial and linguistic skills. In C. Ounsted & D. C. Taylor (Eds.), *Gender differences: Their ontogeny and significance* (pp. 123–158). Edinburgh, UK: Churchill Livingstone.

Burkam, D. T., Lee, V. E., & Smerdon, B. A. (1997). Gender and science learning early in high school: Subject matter and laboratory experiences. *American Educational Research Journal, 34*(2), 297–331.

Burrelli, J. (2008). *Thirty-three years of women in science and engineering faculty positions.* (InfoBrief, NSF 08-308). Arlington, VA: National Science Foundation, Directorate for Social, Behavioral, and Economic Sciences.

Byrne, E. M. (1978). *Women and education.* London, UK: Tavistock.

Bystydzienski, J. M., & Bird, S. R. (Eds.). (2006). *Removing barriers: Women in academic science, technology, engineering and mathematics.* Bloomington, IN: Indiana University Press.

Cheyney University of Pennsylvania. (2012). About CU. Retrieved from http://www.cheyney.edu/about-cheyney-university/

Children's Rights Workshop. (1976). *Sexism in children's books: Facts, figures and guidelines.* London, UK: Writers and Readers Publishing Cooperative.

The Chronicle of Higher Education. (2004, December 3). Where are all the women. *LI*(15). Retrieved from http://chronicle.com/section/Home/5

The Chronicle of Higher Education. (2005a, March 4). Women and science: The debate goes on. *LI*(26). Retrieved from http://chronicle.com/section/Home/5

The Chronicle of Higher Education. (2005b, June 10). The faculty: Women in the national academy. *LI*(40). Retrieved from http://chronicle.com/section/Home/5

Clewell, B. C., & Ginorio, A. B. (2002). Examining women's progress in the sciences from the perspective of diversity. In S. M. Bailey (Ed.), *The Jossey-Bass reader on gender in science* (pp. 609–643). San Francisco, CA: Jossey-Bass.

Cohen, E. (1997). "What the women at all times would laugh at": Redefining equality and difference, circa 1660–1760. In S. G. Kohlstedt & H. E. Longino (Eds.), *Women gender, and science: New directions* (pp. 121–142). Chicago, IL: University of Chicago Press.

Cole, J. R. (1979). *Fair science: Women in the scientific community.* New York, NY: Free Press.

Colley, B. (1999). *Parental involvement at an urban high school: A case study of Robeson High School* (Unpublished doctoral dissertation). Boston College, Chestnut Hill, MA.

Colley, K. E. (2008). Project-based science instruction: A primer. *The Science Teacher, 75*(8), 23-28.

Collins, P. H. (1991). *Black feminist thought: Knowledge, consciousness, and the politics of empowerment.* New York, NY: Routledge.

Coryn, C. L. S., Noakes, L. A., Westine, C. D., & Schroter, D. C. (2011). A systematic review of theory-driven evaluation practice from 1990 to 2009. *American Journal of Evaluation, 32*(2), 199–226.

Czaja, R., & Blair, J. (1996). *Designing surveys: A guide to decisions and procedures.* Thousand Oaks, CA: Pine Forge Press.

Davidson, B. (1984). *Africa in history: Themes and outlines.* London, UK: Paladin Books.

Davidson, B. (1985). *The story of Africa.* London, UK: Mitchell Beazley.

Davis, K. (1995). The participation of women in science: The road less traveled. In D. R. Baker & K. Scantlebury (Eds.), *Science "coeducation": Viewpoints from gender, race and ethnic perspectives* (pp. 178–198). Reston, VA: NARST.

Davis, L., & Meighan, R. (1975). A review of schooling and sex roles with particular reference to the experience of girls in secondary schools. *Educational Review, 27*(3), 165–178.

Delgado, R. (1995). *Critical race theory: The cutting edge.* Philadelphia, PA: Temple University Press.

Delgado, R., & Stefancic, J. (2001). *Critical race theory: An introduction.* New York, NY: New York University Press.

Desy, E. A., Peterson, S. A., & Brockman, V. (2011). Gender differences in science-related attitudes and interests among middle and high school students. *Science Educator, 20*(2), 23–30.

Du Bois, W. E. B. (1903). *The souls of Black folk.* Chicago, IL: A. C. McClurg.

Epstein, J. L. (1995). School-family-community partnership: Caring for the children we share. *Phi Delta Kappan,* May, 701–712.

Evans, S. Y. (2007). *Black women in the ivory tower; 1850–1954.* Gainesville, FL: University Press of Florida.

Ewing, M. S., & Campbell Warner, P. (2002). Wading in the water: Women aquatic biologists coping with clothing, 1877–1945. *BioScience, 52*(1), 97–104.

Fadigan, K. A., & Hammrich, P. L. (2004). A longitudinal study of the educational and career trajectories of female participants in an informal science education program. *Journal of Research in Science Teaching, 41*(8), 835–860.

Fay, B. (1987). *Critical social science: Liberation and its limits.* Ithaca, NY: Cornell University Press.

Ferber, M. A. (2003). Uneven progress in academia: Problems and solutions. In L. S. Horning (Ed.), *Equal rites, unequal outcomes: Women in American research universities* (pp. 281–309). New York, NY: Kluwer Academic/Plenum.

Fleming, M. L., & Malone, M. R. (1983). The relationship of student characteristics and student performance in science as viewed by meta-analysis research. *Journal of Research in Science Teaching, 20*(5), 481–495.

Freeman, M., & Vasconcelos, E. F. S. (2010). Critical social theory: Core tenets, inherent issues. In M. Freeman (Ed.), *Critical social theory and evaluation practice (New directions for evaluation, no. 127)* (pp. 7–19). San Francisco, CA: Wiley/Jossey-Bass.

Freire, P. (1993). *Pedagogy of the oppressed* (Rev. ed.). New York, NY: Continuum.

Friedler, Y., & Tamir, P. (1990). Sex differences in science education in Israel: An analysis of 15 years of research. *Research in Science and Technology Education, 8*(1), 21–34.

Gates, H. L., & McKay, N. Y. (1997). From Phillis Wheatley to Toni Morrison: The flowering of African-American literature. *Journal of Blacks in Higher Education, 14*, 95–100.

Gay, L. R., & Airasian, P. (2000). *Educational research: Competencies for analysis and application.* Upper Saddle River, NJ: Merrill.

Germann, P. J. (1994). Testing a model of science process skills acquisition: An interaction with parents' education, preferred language, gender, science attitude, cognitive development, academic ability, and biology knowledge. *Journal of Research in Science Teaching, 31*(7), 749–783.

Gilbert, J., & Calvert, S. (2003). Challenging accepted wisdom: Looking at the gender and science education question through a different lens. *International Journal of Science Education, 25*(7), 861–878.

Gill, D. (1977). *Illegitimacy, sexuality and the status of women*. London, UK: Blackwell.

Gould, P. (2002). Two good women, or too good to be true? *Science, 296*(5574), 1805–1806.

Gould, S. J. (1996). *The mismeasure of man*. New York, NY: W. W. Norton.

Gray, J. A. (1981). A biological basis for the sex differences in achievement in science? In A. Kelly (Ed.), *The missing half: Girls and science education*. Manchester, UK: Manchester University Press.

Gregory, S. T. (2001). Black faculty women in the academy: History, status, and future. *Journal of Negro Education, 70*(3), 124–138.

Gronim, S. S. (2007). What Jane knew: A woman botanist in the eighteenth century. *Journal of Women's History, 19*(3), 33–59.

Guinier, L., & Torres, G. (2011, October 10). Derrick Bell: The scholar remembered. *The Chronicle Review. The Chronicle of Higher Education*. Retrieved from http://chronicle.com/article/Derrick-Bell-the-Scholar/129339/

Haber, L. (1970). *Black pioneers of science and invention*. New York, NY: Harcourt Brace.

Hamilton, L. S. (1998). Gender differences on high school science achievement tests: Do format and content matter? *Educational Evaluation and Policy Analysis, 20*(3), 179–195.

Hanson, S. L. (2006). African American women in science: Experience from high school through post-secondary years and beyond. In J. M. Bystydzienski & S. R. Bird (Eds.), *Removing barriers: Women in academic science, technology, engineering and mathematics* (pp. 123–141). Bloomington, IN: Indiana University Press.

Harris, R. L (1996). *Information graphics: A comprehensive illustrated reference*. Atlanta, GA: Management Graphics.

Harty, H., Hamrick, L., Ault Jr., C., & Samuel, K. V. (1987). Gender influences on concept structure interrelatedness competence. *Science Education, 71*(1), 105–115.

Hatch, A. R. (2007). Critical race theory. In George Ritzer (Ed.), *Blackwell encyclopedia of sociology*. West Sussex, UK: Wiley-Blackwell, Retrieved from http://www.blackwellreference.com.gate.lib.buffalo.edu/subscriber/tocnode?id=g97814 05124331_chunk_g978140512433319_ss1-207

Haun-Frank, J. (2011). Narratives of identity in everyday spaces: An examination of African American students' science career trajectories. *Science Education International, 22*(4), 239–254.

Herzog, S. E. (Ed.). (1997). *The PTA story: A century of commitment to children*. Marceline, MO: Walsworth.

Hill, S. T., & Johnson, J. M. (2004). Science and engineering degrees, by race/ethnicity of recipients: 1992–2001. (NSF 04-318). Arlington, VA: National Science Foundation, Division of Science Resources Statistics.

Hillsdale College. (2012). History. Retrieved from http://www.hillsdale.edu/

Hohl, E. (2008). *To "uplift ourselves and our race": The new Negro woman of the 1890s* (Unpublished doctoral dissertation). Retrieved from Proquest, Umi Dissertation Publishing.

Horkheimer, M. (1932). Vorwort. *Zeitschrift für Sozialforschung, 1*, i–iv.

Horning, L. S. (Ed.). (2003). *Equal rites, unequal outcomes: Women in American research universities*. New York, NY: Kluwer Academic/Plenum.

Howard-Bostic, C. (2008). Stepping out of the third wave: A contemporary Black feminist paradigm. Retrieved from http://forumonpublicpolicy.com/summer08papers/archivesummer08/howardbostic.pdf

Huguet, P., & Regner, I. (2009). Counter-stereotypic beliefs in math do not protect school girls from stereotype threat. *Journal of Experimental Social Psychology, 45*(4), 1024–1027.

Hyde, J. S. (2005). The gender similarities hypothesis. *American Psychologist, 60*(6), 581–592.

Hyde, J. S., Lindberg, S. M., Linn, M. C., Ellis, A. B., & Williams, C. C. (2008). Gender similarities characterize math performance. *Science, 321*(5888), 494–495.

Jacob, M. C., & Sturkenboom, J. D. (2003). A woman's scientific society in the West: The late eightennth-century assimilation of science. *Isis, 94*(2), 217–252.

John, Bishop of Nikiu. (1916). *The chronicle of John, Bishop of Nikiu* (H. Zotenberg, Ed.; R. H. Charles, Trans.). London, UK: Williams & Norgate.

Johnson, A., Brown, J., Carlone, H., & Cuevas, A. K. (2011). Authoring identity amidst the treacherous terrain of science: A multiracial feminist examination of the journeys of three women of color in science. *Journal of Research in Science Teaching, 48*(4), 339–366.

Jones, B. D. (2002). Critical race theory: New strategies for civil rights in the new millennium? *Harvard BlackLetter Law Journal, 18*, 1–90.

Jones, L. R., Mullis, I. V. S., Raizen, S. A., Weiss, I. R., & Weston, E. A. (1992). The 1990 science report card: NAEP's assessment of fourth, eighth, and twelfth graders. Washington, DC: National Center for Education Statistics.

Jones, M. G., Tretter, T., Paechter, M., Kubasko, D., Bokinsky, A., Andre, T., & Negishi, A. (2007). Differences in African-American and European-American students' engagement with nanotechnology experiences: Perceptual position or assessment artifact? *Journal of Research in Science Teaching 44*(6), 787-799.

Jones, M. G., & Wheatley, J. (1990). Gender differences in teacher-student interactions in science classrooms. *Journal of Research in Science Teaching, 27*(9), 861–874.

Jordan, D. (2006). *Sisters in science*. West Lafayette, IN: Purdue University Press.

Kahle, J. B., Parker, L. H., Rennie, L. J., & Riley, D. (1993). Gender differences in science education: Building a model. *Educational Psychologist, 28*(4), 379–404.

Kang, K. H. (2003). Characteristics of doctoral scientists and engineers in the United States: 2001. (NSF 03-310). Arlington, VA: National Science Foundation, Division of Science Resources Statistics.

Keeves, J. P. (1992). Learning science in a changing world: Cross-national studies of science achievement: 1970 to 1984. The Hague, The Netherlands: International Association for the Evaluation of Educational Achievement.

Keeves, J. P., & Dryden, M. (1992). The teaching and learning of science at population 2: 1983–1984. In J. P. Keeves (Ed.), *The IEA study of science III: Changes in science education and achievement, 1970 to 1984* (pp. 187–207). New York, NY: Pergamon Press.

Keller, E. F. (1996). Feminism and science. In E. F. Keller & H. E. Longino (Eds.), *Feminism and science* (pp. 28–40). Oxford, UK: Oxford University Press.

Kellner, D. (2010). Critical theory and the crisis of social theory. Retrieved from http://www.gseis.ucla.edu/faculty/kellner/kellner.html and http://pages.gseis.ucla.edu/faculty/kellner/essays/criticaltheorycrisisofsocialtheory.pdf

Kelly, A. (1976). Women in physics and physics education. In J. Lewis (Ed.), *New trends in physics teaching, Vol. III* (pp. 241–266). Paris, France: UNESCO. Retrieved from http://unesdoc.unesco.org/images/0013/001368/136807eo.pdf

Kelly, E. (1981). Socialisation in patriarchal society. In A. Kelly (Ed.), *The missing half: Girls and science education* (pp. 59–72). Manchester, UK: Manchester University Press.

Kohlstedt, S. G., & Longino, H. E. (1997). The women, gender, and science question: What do research on women in science and research on gender and science have to do with each other? In S. G. Kohlstedt & H. E. Longino (Eds.), *Women, gender, and science: New directions* (pp. 3–15). Chicago, IL: University of Chicago Press.

Ladson-Billings, G., & Tate, W. F. (1995). Toward a critical race theory of education. *Teachers College Record, 97*(1), 47–68.

Langenheim, J. H. (1996). Early history and progress of women ecologists: Emphasis upon research contributions. *Annual Review of Ecology and Systematics, 27*(1), 1–53.

Leach, C. (2006). Religion and rationality: Quaker women and science education 1790-1850. *History of Education, 35*(1), 69-90.

Lee, V., Marks, H., & Knowles, T. (1991, August). *Sexism in single-sex and coeducational secondary school classrooms.* Paper presented at the annual meeting of the American Sociological Association, Cincinnati, OH.

Lewis, J. L., Menzies, H., Nájera, E. I., & Page, R. N. (2009). Rethinking trends in minority participation in the sciences. *Science Education, 93*(6), 961–977.

Ley, T. J., & Hamilton, B. H. (2008). The gap in NIH grant applications. *Science, 332*(5907), 1472–1474.

Linn, M. C., De Benedictis, T., Delucchi, K., Harris, A., & Stage, E. (1987). Gender differences in national assessment of educational progress science items: What does "I don't know" really mean? *Journal of Research in Science Teaching, 24*(3), 267–278.

Lipsitz Bem, S. (1993). *The lenses of gender: Transforming the debate on sexual equality.* New Haven, CT: Yale University Press.

Litwack, L. F. (1998). The White man's fear of the educated Negro: How the Negro was fitted for his natural and logical calling. *Journal of Blacks in Higher Education, 20*, 100–108.

Lumpkin, B. (1997). Hypatia and women's rights in ancient Egypt. In I. Van Sertima (Ed.), *Black women in antiquity* (pp. 155–161). London, UK: Transaction.

Matyas, M. L. (1991). Women, minorities and persons with physical disabilities in science and engineering: Contributing factors and study methodology. In M. L. Matyas & S. M. Malcom (Eds.), *Investing in human potential: Science and engineering at the crossroads* (pp. 13–36). Washington, DC: American Association for the Advancement of Science.

Mayer, W. J., & Thompson, G. G. (1963). Teacher-interaction with boys as contrasted with girls. In R. G. Kuhlens & G. G. Thompson (Eds.), *Psychological studies of human development* (pp.). New York, NY: Appleton-Century-Crofts.

M'Bow, A-M. (1990). Preface. In G. Mokhtar (Ed.), *General history of Africa II: Ancient civilizations of African prehistory* (Abridged ed., pp. vii–xi). UNESCO International Scientific Committee for the Drafting of a General History of Africa. Paris, France: UNESCO.

McComas, W. F. (2004). Keys to teaching the nature of science. *Science Teacher, 71*(9), 24–27.

McRobbie, A. (1978). Working class girls and the culture of femininity. In Women's Studies Group, CCCS (Ed.), *Women take issue: Aspects of women's subordination* (pp. 96–108). London, UK: Hutchinson.

Minner, D. D., Levy, A. J., & Century, J. (2010). Inquiry-based science instruction—What is it and does it matter? Results from a research synthesis years 1984 to 2002. *Journal of Research in Science Teaching, 47*(4), 474–496.

Mokros, J., & Tinker, R. (1987). The impact of microcomputer-based labs on children's ability to interpret graphs. *Journal of Research in Science Teaching, 24*, 369–383.

Mullis, I. V. S., Dossey, J. A., Campbell, J. R., Gentile, C. A., O'Sullivan, C. O., & Latham, A. S. (1994). NEAP 1992, Trends in academic progress: Achievement of U.S. students in science, mathematics, 1973 to 1992; reading, 1971 to 1992; writing, 1984 to 1992. Washington, DC: Office of Education Research and Improvement, United States Department of Education.

Mullis, I. V. S., Martin, M. O., Beaton, A. E., Gonzalez, E. J., Kelly, D. L., & Smith, T. A. (1998). Mathematics and science achievement in the final years of secondary school: IEA's third international mathematics and science study. Chestnut Hill, MA: TIMSS International Study Center, Boston College.

National Academies. (2010). *Gender differences at critical transitions in the careers of science, engineering, and mathematics faculty.* Washington, DC: Author.

National Academy of Sciences. (2010). Expanding underrepresented minority participation: America's science and technology talent at the crossroads. Washington, DC: National Academies Press.

National Academy of Sciences. (2007). *Beyond bias and barriers: Fulfilling the potential of women in academic science and engineering.* Washington, DC: National Academies Press.

National Assessment of Educational Progress (NAEP). (1978a). *Science achievement in the schools: A summary of results from the 1976–1977 national assessment of science.* (Report # 08-S-01). Denver, CO: Education Commission of the States.

National Assessment of Educational Progress (NAEP). (1978b). *Three national assessments of science: Changes in achievement, 1969–1977.* (Report # 08-S-00). Denver, CO: Education Commission of the States.

National Assessment of Educational Progress (NAEP). (1979a). *Attitudes towards science: A summary of results from the 1969–1977 national assessment of science.* (Report # 08-S-02). Denver, CO: Education Commission of the States.

National Assessment of Educational Progress (NAEP). (1979b). *Three national assessments of science, 1969–1977: Technical summary.* (Report # 08-S-21). Denver, CO: Education Commission of the States.

National Center for Education Statistics (NCES). (2012). *Nation report card 2011.* Washington, DC: Author.

National Research Council. (1981). *Postdoctoral appointments and disappointments. A report of the committee on a study of postdoctorals in science and engineering in the United States, Commission on Human Resources.* Washington, DC: National Academy Press.

National Research Council. (1996). *National science education standards.* Washington, DC: National Academy Press.

National Research Council. (2006). *To recruit and advance women students and faculty in science and engineering.* Washington DC: National Academy Press.

National Science Foundation (NSF). (1990). *Future scarcities of scientists and engineers: Problems and solutions.* Directorate for Scientific, Technological, and International Affairs, Division of Policy Research and Analysis. (Working Draft, Summer 1990). Washington, DC: National Science Foundation.

National Science Foundation (NSF). (2004a). *Gender differences in the careers of academic scientists and engineers.* (NSF 04-323). Arlington, VA: Division of Science Resources Statistics.

National Science Foundation (NSF). (2004b). *Science and engineering degrees, by race/ethnicity of recipients: 1992–2001.* (NSF 04-318). Arlington, VA: Division of Science Resources Statistics.

National Science Foundation (NSF). (2007). *Women, minorities, and persons with disabilities in science and engineering.* (NSF 07-315). Arlington, VA: Division of Science Resources Statistics.

National Science Foundation (NSF). (2008). TABLE 9-39 Demographic characteristics of employed scientists and engineers, by race/ethnicity and sex: 2008. Arlington, VA: National Science Foundation, National Center for Science and Engineering Statistics.

National Science Foundation (NSF). (2009). *Women, minorities, and persons with disabilities in science and engineering: 2009.* Arlington, VA: Author.

National Science Foundation (NSF). (2010). *TABLE 9-22 Science, engineering, and health doctorate holders employed in universities and 4-year colleges, by type of academic position, sex, race/ethnicity, and disability status: 2010.* Arlington, VA: National Science Foundation, National Center for Science and Engineering Statistics.

National Science Foundation (NSF). (2011). *Women, minorities, and persons with disabilities in science and engineering.* Arlington, VA: Division of Science Resources Statistics.

Norman, O., Ault, C. R. Jr., Bentz, B., & Meskimen, L. (2001). The Black-White "Achievement Gap" as a perennial challenge of urban science education: A sociocultural and historical overview with implications for research and practice. *Journal of Research in Science Teaching 38*(10), 1101–1114.

Oberlin University. (2012). About Oberlin. Retrieved from http://new.oberlin.edu/about/index.dot

Rapoport, A. I. (2004). Gender differences in the careers of academic scientists and engineers. (NSF 04-323). Arlington, VA: National Science Foundation, Division of Science Resources Statistics.

Ridley, G. (2010). *The discovery of Jeanne Baret.* New York, NY: Crown.

Rivet, A. E., & Krajcik, J. S. (2004). Achieving standards in urban systemic reform: An example of a sixth grade project-based science curriculum. *Journal of Research in Science Teaching, 41*(7), 669–692.

Robinson, R. (2000). The debt: *What America owes to Blacks.* New York, NY: Dutton.

Russell, M. L., & Atwater, M. M. (2005). Traveling the road to success: A discourse on persistence throughout the science pipeline with African American students at a predominantly White institution. *Journal of Research in Science Teaching, 42*(6), 691–715.

Sadker, M., & Sadker, D. (1986). Sexism in the classroom: From grade school to graduate school. *Phi Delta Kappan, 67*(7), 512–515.

Sadler, T. D., Burgin, S., McKinney, L., & Ponjuan, L. (2010). Learning science through research apprenticeships: A critical review of the literature. *Journal of Research in Science Teaching, 47*(3), 235–256.

Sanchez, S. (1997). Nefertiti: Queen to a sacred mission. In I. Van Sertima (Ed.), *Black women in antiquity* (pp. 49–55). London, UK: Transaction.

Saraga, E., & Griffiths, D. (1981). Biological inevitabilities or political choices? The future for girls in science. In A. Kelly (Ed.), *The missing half: Girls and science education* (pp. 85–99). Manchester, UK: Manchester University Press.

SAS Institute. (2002). JMP statistical discovery software. Version 5.1. Cary, NC: Author.

Sears, R. S., & Feldman, D. H. (1974). Teacher interactions with boys and with girls. In J. Stacey, S. Bereaud, & J. Daniels (Eds.), *And Jill came tumbling after: Sexism in American education* (pp. 147–158). New York, NY: Dell.

Settles, I. H., Cortina, L. M., Malley, J., & Stewart, A. J. (2006). The climate for women in academic science: The good, the bad, and the changeable. *Psychology of Women Quarterly, 30*(1), 47–58.

Sharpe, S. (1976). *Just like a girl: How girls learn to be women.* London, UK: Pelican Books.

Shavelson, R. J. (1972). Some aspects of the correspondence between content structure and cognitive structure in physics instruction. *Journal of Educational Psychology, 63*(3), 225–234.

Shavelson, R. J., & Stanton, G. C. (1975). Construct validation: Methodology and application to three measures of cognitive structure. *Journal of Educational Measurement, 12*(2), 67–85.

Shteir, A. B. (1996). *Cultivating women, cultivating science: Flora's daughters and botany in Englamd, 1760 to 1860.* Baltimore, MD: Johns Hopkins University Press.

Small, B., & Kelly, A. (1984a). Sex differences in science and technology among 11-year-old schoolchildren: I—Cognitive. *Research in Science and Technology Education, 2*(1), 61–76.

Small, B., & Kelly, A. (1984b). Sex differences in science and technology among 11-year-old schoolchildren: II—Affective. *Research in Science and Technology Education, 2*(2), 87–106.

Sonnert, G., & Holton, G. (1995). *Who succeeds in science? The gender dimension.* New Brunswick, NJ: Rutgers University Press.

Sorge, C. (2007). What happens? Relationship of age and gender with science attitudes from elementary to middle school. *Science Educator, 16*(2), 33–37.

Stacey, J., Bereaud, S., & Daniels. J. (Eds.). (1974). *And Jill came tumbling after: Sexism in American education.* New York, NY: Dell.

Stake, R. E. (2010). *Qualitative research: Studying how things work.* New York, NY: Guilford Press.

Stanworth, M. (1983). *Gender and schooling: A study of sexual divisions in the classroom.* London, UK: Hutchinson.

Staver, J. R., & Walberg, H. J. (1986). An analysis of factors that affect public and private school science achievement. *Journal of Research in Science Teaching, 23*(2), 97–112.

Steinkamp, M. W., & Maehr, M. L. (1983). Affect, ability, and science achievement: A quantitative synthesis of correlational research. *Review of Educational Research, 53*(3), 369–396.

Stephey, M. J. (2008). A brief history of tenure. Retrieved on April 11, 2013 from http://www.time.com/time/nation/article/0,8599,1859505,00.html

Stewart, M. W. (1972). Teaching school to keep alive. In G. Lerner (Ed.), *Black women in White America* (pp. 83 -84). New York, NY: Vintage Books.

Strauss, A. L., & Corbin, J. M. (1990). *Basics of qualitative research: Grounded theory procedures and techniques.* Newbury Park, CA: Sage.

Tate, W. F. (1997). Critical race theory and education: History, theory, and implications. *Review of Research in Education, 22*(1), 195–247.

Thomas, D. R. (2006). A general inductive approach for analyzing qualitative evaluation data. *American Journal of Evaluation, 27*(2), 237–246.

Thomas, G. D., & Hollenshead, C. (2001). Resisting from the margins: The coping strategies of Black women and other women of color faculty members at a research university. *Journal of Negro Education, 70*(3), 166–175.

Titcomb, C. (1997). The earliest Ph.D. awards to Blacks in the natural sciences. *Journal of Blacks in Higher Education, 14*, 95–100.

Tobin, K., & Garnett, P. (1987). Gender related differences in science activities. *Science Education, 71*(1), 91–103.

Unah, J. I., & Dennis, O. (2011). Simone de Beauvoir's philosophical sexism: Implications for the philosophy of posterity. Retrieved from http://forumonpublicpolicy.com/vol2011no3/archive/unah.pdf

Van Lawick-Goodall, J. (1968). The behaviour of free-living chimpanzees in the Gombe Stream Reserve. *Animal Behavior Monograph, 1*, 161–311.

Van Sertima, I. (Ed.). (1997). *Black women in antiquity.* London, UK: Transaction.

Van Sertima, I. (Ed.). (1998). *Blacks in science: Ancient and modern.* New Brunswick, NJ: Transaction.

Warren, W. (1999). *Black women scientists in the United States.* Bloomington, IN: Indiana University Press.

West, M. S., & Curtis, J. W. (2006). AAUP faculty gender indicators 2006. Washington, DC: American Association of University Professors (AAUP).

Wilberforce University. (2013). About WU. Retrieved from http://www.wilberforce.edu/administration/index.html

Wimby, D. (1997). The female horuses and great wives of Kemet. In I. Van Sertima (Ed.), *Black women in antiquity* (pp. 36–48). London, UK: Transaction.

Wolpe, A-M. (1977). *Some processes in sexist education. Explorations in Feminism, No. 1.* Atlanta, GA: Women's Research and Resource Center.

Yasso, T. J. (2005). Whose culture has capital? A critical race theory discussion of community cultural wealth. *Race, Ethnicity and Education, 8*(1), 69–91.

Yentsch, C. M., & Sindermann, C. J. (1992). *The woman scientist: Meeting the challenges for a successful career.* New York, NY: Plenum Press.

Zahra, H., Tai, R. H., & Sadler, P. M. (2007). Gender differences in introductory university physics performance: The influence of high school physics preparation and affective factors. *Science Education, 91*(6), 847–876.

Index

ROCHELLE BROCK &
RICHARD GREGGORY JOHNSON III,
Executive Editors

Black Studies and Critical Thinking is an interdisciplinary series which examines the intellectual traditions of and cultural contributions made by people of African descent throughout the world. Whether it is in literature, art, music, science, or academics, these contributions are vast and far-reaching. As we work to stretch the boundaries of knowledge and understanding of issues critical to the Black experience, this series offers a unique opportunity to study the social, economic, and political forces that have shaped the historic experience of Black America, and that continue to determine our future. Black Studies and Critical Thinking is positioned at the forefront of research on the Black experience, and is the source for dynamic, innovative, and creative exploration of the most vital issues facing African Americans. The series invites contributions from all disciplines but is specially suited for cultural studies, anthropology, history, sociology, literature, art, and music.

Subjects of interest include (but are not limited to):

- EDUCATION
- SOCIOLOGY
- HISTORY
- MEDIA/COMMUNICATION
- RELIGION/THEOLOGY
- WOMEN'S STUDIES

- POLICY STUDIES
- ADVERTISING
- AFRICAN AMERICAN STUDIES
- POLITICAL SCIENCE
- LGBT STUDIES

For additional information about this series or for the submission of manuscripts, please contact Dr. Brock (Indiana University Northwest) at brock2@iun.edu or Dr. Johnson (University of San Francisco) at rgjohnsoniii@usfca.edu.

To order other books in this series, please contact our Customer Service Department:

(800) 770-LANG (within the U.S.)
(212) 647-7706 (outside the U.S.)
(212) 647-7707 FAX

Or browse online by series at www.peterlang.com.